Anne Boleyn

Anne Boleyn. (*After John Hoskins*)

Anne Boleyn

An Illustrated Life of Henry VIII's Queen

Roland Hui

First published in Great Britain in 2023 by
Pen & Sword History
An imprint of
Pen & Sword Books Ltd
Yorkshire – Philadelphia

Copyright © Roland Hui 2023

ISBN 978 1 39908 757 5

The right of Roland Hui to be identified as Author of this work has been asserted by him in accordance with the Copyright, Designs and Patents Act 1988.

A CIP catalogue record for this book is
available from the British Library.

All rights reserved. No part of this book may be reproduced or transmitted in any form or by any means, electronic or mechanical including photocopying, recording or by any information storage and retrieval system, without permission from the Publisher in writing.

Typeset by Mac Style
Printed in the UK by CPI Group (UK) Ltd, Croydon, CR0 4YY.

Pen & Sword Books Limited incorporates the imprints of Atlas, Archaeology, Aviation, Discovery, Family History, Fiction, History, Maritime, Military, Military Classics, Politics, Select, Transport, True Crime, Air World, Frontline Publishing, Leo Cooper, Remember When, Seaforth Publishing, The Praetorian Press, Wharncliffe Local History, Wharncliffe Transport, Wharncliffe True Crime and White Owl.

For a complete list of Pen & Sword titles please contact

PEN & SWORD BOOKS LIMITED
47 Church Street, Barnsley, South Yorkshire, S70 2AS, England
E-mail: enquiries@pen-and-sword.co.uk
Website: www.pen-and-sword.co.uk

Or

PEN AND SWORD BOOKS
1950 Lawrence Rd, Havertown, PA 19083, USA
E-mail: Uspen-and-sword@casematepublishers.com
Website: www.penandswordbooks.com

Contents

List of Illustrations	vii
Prologue	xiv
Part I	1
Chapter 1	3
Chapter 2	15
Chapter 3	31
Chapter 4	47
Part II	55
Chapter 5	57
Chapter 6	68
Chapter 7	76
Chapter 8	85
Part III	95
Chapter 9	97
Chapter 10	106
Chapter 11	112
Chapter 12	124
Part IV	137
Chapter 13	139
Chapter 14	147
Chapter 15	161
Chapter 16	170
Epilogue	177
Notes and Sources	182
Bibliography	194
Index	198

Reviews for *Anne Boleyn: An Illustrated Life (by Roland Hui)*

'A gem of a book, painting an absorbing and sparkling portrait of Anne Boleyn, with lavish illustrations and documentations. A must-read for Tudor enthusiasts.'
Margaret George, author of *The Autobiography of Henry VIII: With Notes by His Fool, Will Somers*

'Richly illustrated and full of fascinating detail, this is a Tudor book to treasure. Fabulous!'
Leanda de Lisle, author of *Tudor: The Family Story*

'The story of Anne Boleyn's life and death comes vividly to life in this illustrated biography. Enlivened with illustrations of people, places and objects intimately connected with Anne's story, this book is a must-read for Tudor enthusiasts.'
Sylvia Barbara Soberton, author of *Ladies-in-Waiting: Women Who Served Anne Boleyn*

'Roland Hui's lavishly illustrated new biography is a must for every Anne Boleyn fan. Hui manages to make seemingly familiar material feel fresh and new, and the emphasis on Anne's early years and education is welcome. A compelling, lively biography.'
Stephanie Russo, author of *The Afterlife of Anne Boleyn: Representations of Anne Boleyn in Fiction and on the Screen*

'Roland Hui has an eye for detail and a way of writing prose that is both authoritative and compulsively readable. This illustrated history puts Anne Boleyn's life in context - her world fleshed out alongside the stunning artwork of the period. Absorbing and meticulous, this is a book you won't want to miss.'
Adrienne Dillard, author of *Keeper of the Queen's Jewels*

'This is a treasure of a book: beautifully written, sumptuously illustrated, and deeply moving. Compulsive reading even for seasoned fans of Anne Boleyn and the Tudor dynasty.'
Steven Veerapen, author of *Elizabeth and Essex: Power, Passion, and Politics*

List of Illustrations

Frontispiece: Anne Boleyn (*By an Unknown Artist after John Hoskins*). ii
1. Brass of Sir Thomas Boleyn. (Illustration from Charles Knight's *The Popular History of England*, 1864). Private Collection. 3
2. Blickling Hall in the Nineteenth Century. (*By James Baylis Allen after John Preston Neale*). Private Collection. 5
3. Coin of King Ferdinand and Queen Isabella of Spain. The National Gallery of Art, Washington D.C., Samuel H. Kress Collection. 6
4. Saint Paul's Cathedral. (*By Wenceslaus Hollar*). The Metropolitan Museum of Art, New York, Gift of Leo Steinberg, 1991. 7
5. Hever Castle in the Eighteenth Century. (*By Samuel and Nathaniel Buck*). Private Collection. 8
6. Christ in the Rosary. (*School of Dürer*). The Rijksmuseum, Amsterdam. 10
7. Margaret of Austria. (*By Bernard van Orley*). The Royal Museum of Fine Arts, Antwerp. 11
8. Emperor Maximilian Receiving Margaret of Austria and His Grandchildren. (*By Hans Burgkmair*). The Metropolitan Museum of Art, New York, Harris Brisbane Dick Fund, 1943. 12
9. The Court of Cambrai (the Keizershof) as it was in 1500. (*By August van den Eynde*). © Stadsarchief Mechelen – City Archives Mechelen. 15
10. Don Diégo de Guevara(?). (*By Michel Sittow*). The National Gallery of Art, Washington D.C., Andrew W. Mellon Collection. 16
11. Castle Tervuren in La Veure (from Antonius Sanderus's *Chorographia Sacra Brabantiae*). The Rijksmuseum, Amsterdam. 17

12. The Arrival of the Statue of Notre Dame du Sablon in Brussels, detail. (*By Bernard van Orley*). © Royal Museums of Art and History, Brussels. 19
13. Mechelen. (*By Georg Braun and Franz Hogenberg in* Civitates orbis terrarum). © Stadsarchief Mechelen – City Archives Mechelen. 20
14. The Court of Savoy in the Nineteenth Century. (*By Jan Baptist De Noter*). © Stadsarchief Mechelen – City Archives Mechelen. 23
15. Emperor Maximilian from the Choirbook of Margaret of Austria. (*Attributed to Gerard Horenbout*). © Stadsarchief Mechelen – City Archives Mechelen. 24
16. The Coudenberg Palace. (*By Jan van de Velde*). The Rijksmuseum, Amsterdam. 26
17. Altarpiece with Christian II and Isabeau of Austria. (*By an Unknown Artist*). Courtesy of The National Museum of Denmark, photo by Lennart Larsen. 28
18. Medal of Louis XII. (*By an Unknown Artist*). The National Gallery of Art, Washington D.C., Widener Collection. 29
19. The City and Memorable Abbey of Saint Denis. (*By Claude Chastillon in* Topographie françoise). INHA Digital Library. 31
20. Paris. (*By Léonard Gaultier*). Private Collection. 33
21. Renée of France. (*From Guillaume Rouillé's* La seconde partie du proptuaire de medalles, *1577*). Private Collection. 34
22. Mary, Queen of France and Charles Brandon, Duke of Suffolk. (*By George Vertue after an Unknown Artist*). The Yale Center for British Art, In Memory of Jeanne and Paul Rapoport. 35
23. The Castle Royal in the Forest of Vincennes. (*By an Unknown Artist*). Private Collection. 36
24. Queen Claude. (*By an Unknown Artist*). Private Collection. 38
25. Francis I. (*Workshop of Joos Van Cleve*). The Metropolitan Museum of Art, New York, The Friedsam Collection, Bequest of Michael Friedsam, 1931. 38
26. Henry VIII. (*By Cornelis Anthonisz*). The Rijksmuseum, Amsterdam. 40
27. The Field of the Cloth of Gold. (*By Edward Edwards and James Basire after an Unknown Artist*). The Yale Center for British Art, Yale University Art Gallery Collection. 42

List of Illustrations   ix

28. Katherine of Aragon. (*By G.P. Harding after an Unknown Artist*). The Folger Shakespeare Library.   44
29. Cardinal Thomas Wolsey. (*By Renold Elstrack*). The National Gallery of Art, Washington D.C., Rosenwald Collection.   47
30. James Butler. (*By Hans Holbein*). Photograph from The Rijksmuseum, Amsterdam.   49
31. Anne Boleyn. (*By an Unknown Artist*). Courtesy of Lyndhurst Mansion, New York.   51
32. Sir Thomas Wyatt. (*By Francesco Bartolozzi after Hans Holbein*). The Cleveland Museum of Art.   53
33. Medal of Charles V. (*By Hans Reinhart the Elder*). The National Gallery of Art, Washington D.C., Samuel H. Kress Collection.   57
34. Whitehall Palace, Formerly York Place. (*By Wenceslaus Hollar*). The Rijksmuseum, Amsterdam.   59
35. King Henry the Eighth and Anna Bullen. (*By William Hogarth*). The Metropolitan Museum of Art, New York.   62
36. A Courtly Couple. (*By Hans Holbein*). The Kunstmuseum, Basel.   65
37. Henry Fitzroy, Duke of Richmond. (*By Harding and Clamp after Lucas Horenbout*). Private Collection.   66
38. Reginald Pole, Later Archbishop of Canterbury. (*By Pieter van Gunst after Adriaen van der Werff*). The Rijksmuseum, Amsterdam.   69
39. Medal of Henry VIII in 1526. (*By Hans Daucher*). The National Gallery of Art, Washington D.C., Samuel H. Kress Collection.   70
40. Self Portrait. (*By Hans Holbein*). Courtesy of The Indianapolis Museum of Art at Newfields.   71
41. The Ball. (*By Cornelis Anthonisz*). The Rijksmuseum, Amsterdam.   73
42. Medal of Pope Clement VII (by an Unknown Artist). The National Gallery of Art, Washington D.C., Samuel H. Kress Collection.   75
43. The Siege of Castel Sant'Angelo in Rome, 1527. (*By Dirck Volckertsz*). The Rijksmuseum, Amsterdam.   75
44. William Warham, Archbishop of Canterbury. (*By Francesco Bartolozzi after Hans Holbein*). The Cleveland Museum of Art.   77

45. Sir William Fitzwilliam. (*By Francesco Bartolozzi after Hans Holbein*). The Yale Center for British Art, Paul Mellon Collection. 78
46. Richmond Palace. (*By Wenceslaus Hollar*). The Metropolitan Museum of Art, New York, Rogers Fund, 1920. 79
47. Stephen Gardiner, Bishop of Winchester. (*By Sylvester Harding and W.N. Gardiner*). The Folger Shakespeare Library. 80
48. Greenwich Palace. (*By James Basire after an Unknown Artist*). The Yale Center for British Art, Paul Mellon Collection. 81
49. Sir William Butts. (*By Hans Holbein*). Photogravure by C.W. Beck in The Wellcome Collection. 82
50. William Carey. (*By an Unknown Artist*). Image courtesy of the National Portrait Gallery, London. 83
51. Cardinal Lorenzo Campeggio. (*By Edward Harding*). The Folger Shakespeare Library. 85
52. Bridewell Palace. (*By Johannes Kip*). The Yale Center for British Art, Paul Mellon Collection. 87
53. The Family of Henry VII at Worship. (*By Charles Grignion after an Unknown Artist*). The Folger Shakespeare Library. 89
54. The Death of Richard Hunne. (*From John Foxe's* Acts and Monuments). Private Collection. 90
55. Martin Luther. (*By Lucas Cranach*). The Nationalmuseum, Sweden. 92
56. *The Obedience of a Christian Man.* (*By William Tyndale*). The Folger Shakespeare Library. 93
57. Thomas Howard, Third Duke of Norfolk. (*By Lucas Vorsterman after Hans Holbein*). The Metropolitan Museum of Art, New York, The Elisha Whittelsey Collection, The Elisha Whittelsey Fund, 1951. 97
58. Sir Thomas More. (*After Hans Holbein*). The Cleveland Museum of Art. 98
59. Eustace Chapuys. (*By an Unknown Artist*). Private Collection. 100
60. Thomas Cranmer, Archbishop of Canterbury. (*By William Holl after Gerlach Flicke*). The Folger Shakespeare Library. 102
61. Thomas Cromwell. (*By an Unknown Artist*). Courtesy of The Indianapolis Museum of Art at Newfields. 104

List of Illustrations   xi

62. Sir Henry Guildford. *(By Wenceslaus Hollar after Hans Holbein)*. The Yale University Art Gallery, New Haven.   104
63. Windsor Castle. (*By Wenceslaus Hollar*). The Rijksmuseum, Amsterdam.   105
64. A View of Hampton Court as Finished by K. Henry VIII. (*By John Pye after Wenceslaus Hollar*). The Yale Center for British Art, Paul Mellon Collection.   106
65. Calais in the 16th Century. (*By an Unknown Artist*). Private Collection.   108
66. Eleanor of Austria, Queen of France. (*By Cornelis Anthonisz*). The Rijksmuseum, Amsterdam.   110
67. The Marriage of Henry VIII and Anne Boleyn. (*By Christian Gottlieb Geyser after Daniel Nikolaus Chodowiecki*). The Rijksmuseum, Amsterdam.   113
68. The Ruins of Walsingham Abbey in the 18th Century. (*By Gerard Vandergucht after J. Badslade in* Vetusta Monumenta). Private Collection.   114
69. Lady Mary Howard, Later Duchess of Richmond and Somerset. (*By Francesco Bartolozzi after Hans Holbein*). The Metropolitan Museum of Art, New York, Gift of Mrs. Thomas T. Gaunt, 1942.   115
70. Anne Boleyn's Device of the White Falcon. (*By an Unknown Artist*). Private Collection.   115
71. The Tower of London, detail. (*After William Haiward and John Gascoyne, 1597*). Private Collection.   117
72. Westminster Abbey. (*By Wenceslaus Hollar*). The University of Toronto Wenceslas Hollar Digital Collection.   119
73. The Great Comet of 1533. (*By Nicolaus Prueckner*). Private Collection.   120
74. Illustration of *The Boleyn Cup* from The Church of St. John the Baptist, Cirencester. (*By an Unknown Artist*). Private Collection.   122
75. The Boleyn Cup. (*By Hans Holbein*). The Kunstmuseum, Basel.   124
76. Design for a Table Fountain. (*By Hans Holbein*). The Kunstmuseum, Basel.   127
77. Woodcut of Anne Boleyn's 1534 Medal. (*From Edward Hawkins'* Medallic Illustrations, *1885*). Private Collection.   128

78. The Lady of the Garter. (*By Lucas Horenbout in* The Black Book of the Garter, *1534*). The Deans and Canons of Windsor, St. George's Chapel Archives & Chapter Library. 130
79. Unknown Lady, Perhaps Mary Boleyn. (*Attributed to Lucas Horenbout*). Courtesy of The Royal Ontario Museum, © ROM. 131
80. Princess Mary. (*By Wenceslaus Hollar after Hans Holbein*). The Rijksmuseum, Amsterdam. 133
81. Philippe Chabot, Admiral De Brion. (*By an Unknown Artist*). Private Collection. 134
82. John Fisher, Bishop of Rochester. (*By Philip Galle*). Private Collection. 139
83. Acton Court in the 19th Century. (*By P. Oushton*). Library of Congress Prints and Photographs Division Washington, D.C. 140
84. Sir Nicholas Poyntz. (*By Hans Holbein*). Photograph from The Rijksmuseum, Amsterdam. 141
85. Margaret of Angoulême. (*From Theodore Beza's* Les vrais pourtraits des hommes illustrés, *1581*). Private Collection. 142
86. Nicholas Bourbon. (*By Francesco Bartolozzi after Hans Holbein*). The Metropolitan Museum of Art, New York, Gift of Mrs. Thomas T. Gaunt, 1942. 143
87. Title Page of The English Bible with *HA* cipher, 1535. Private Collection. 145
88. William Tyndale. (*By François van Bleyswijck*). The Rijksmuseum, Amsterdam. 146
89. King Solomon and the Queen of Sheba. (*By Wenceslaus Hollar after Hans Holbein*). The Rijksmuseum, Amsterdam. 148
90. The Entry of Charles V and Pope Clement VII into Bologna. (*By Nicolaas Hogenberg*). The Rijksmuseum, Amsterdam. 150
91. Jane Seymour. (*By Nicholas Hilliard*). The Nationalmuseum, Sweden. 152
92. Sir Edward Seymour. (*By Jacob Houbraken*). The Rijksmuseum, Amsterdam. 153
93. Sir Nicholas Carew. (*By Hans Holbein*). The Kunstmuseum, Basel. 154

94. Procession of the Knights of the Garter. *(By Joseph Sympson after Lucas Horenbout in* The Black Book of the Garter, *1534).* Private Collection. 155
95. Queen Esther Before King Ahasuerus. *(By Lucas van Leyden).* The Cleveland Museum of Art. 156
96. Hatfield House in the 18th Century. *(By Francesco Sesone).* The Rijksmuseum, Amsterdam. 158
97. Matthew Parker. *(By George Vertue after an Unknown Artist).* The Folger Shakespeare Library. 159
98. Sir William Paulet. *(By an Unknown Artist).* The Yale Center for British Art, Paul Mellon Collection. 162
99. The Tower of London. *(By Wenceslaus Hollar).* The Cleveland Museum of Art. 164
100. Westminster from the River. *(By Wenceslaus Hollar).* The Metropolitan Museum of Art, New York, Harris Brisbane Dick Fund, 1917. 166
101. Henry Howard, Earl of Surrey. *(By Wenceslaus Hollar after Hans Holbein).* The Rijksmuseum, Amsterdam. 168
102. Lambeth Palace. *(By Wenceslaus Hollar).* The Metropolitan Museum of Art, New York, Harris Brisbane Dick Fund, 1917. 171
103. The White Tower. *(By William Woolnoth after W. Winkle).* The Yale Center for British Art, Paul Mellon Collection. 173
104. The Execution of Anne Boleyn. *(By an Unknown Artist).* The Rijksmuseum, Amsterdam. 175
105. Allegory of the Tudor Succession. *(By an Unknown Artist after Lucas de Heere).* The Yale Center for British Art, Paul Mellon Collection. 178
106. The Funeral Procession of Queen Elizabeth. *(By James Basire after William Camden).* The Wellcome Collection. 180

Cover credits: *Anne Boleyn* by an Unknown Artist, Lyndhurst Mansion, New York; *Henry VIII* by Nicholas Hilliard, Nationalmuseum Stockholm; *King Henry the Eighth and Anna Bullen* by William Hogarth, The Metropolitan Museum of Art, New York; *Henry VIII of England Courting Anne Boleyn* by Jules David, The Rijksmuseum, Amsterdam.

Prologue

Among the surviving letters of Thomas Cromwell, the great minister of King Henry VIII, was one addressed from Sir Thomas Boleyn, Earl of Wiltshire. Written in July 1536, Boleyn was responding to a request from the king regarding a financial settlement. While the correspondence was purely business, Boleyn could not help but include a personal reminiscence. As a young man, he told Cromwell, he was living on £50 pounds (about £33,300 today) a year to support himself and his growing family.

Although the recollection was meant to point out his former livelihood, surely it brought back memories of happier times to Thomas Boleyn. The year 1536 was an *annus horribilis* in which his world had unexpectedly and suddenly collapsed around him. He had lost the king's favour, and with that, his much-valued position at court. But more terribly, two of Boleyn's children were put to death on charges of high treason. Incredibly, one was the Queen of England herself.

Part I

'I find her so bright and pleasant for her young age, that I am more beholden to you for sending her to me than you are to me.'

Margaret of Austria to Sir Thomas Boleyn, 1513

Chapter 1

The Boleyn–Howard match was most fruitful. According to Sir Thomas's remembrances, his wife had provided him 'every year a child'. The date of his marriage to Elizabeth Howard is vague, but it was sometime around 1498 when he was about 21. At least five children were produced: Mary, George, Anne, and two boys, Thomas and Henry, who both died young. According to the Elizabethan antiquarian William Camden, their daughter Anne was born in 1507. This claim was backed up by Jane Dormer, a lady-in-waiting to Queen Mary I and later Duchess of Feria, who went on record saying that at the time of her death in 1536, Anne Boleyn was 'not 29 years of age'. The seventeenth-century historian and politician, Sir Roger Twysden, concurred when he stated in his biography of Anne that she was 'not above 7 years of age' in the year 1514 when she went to France, and that 'Anne was born 1507'. Twysden was a good authority as his book was derived from an unpublished life of her written by his uncle George Wyatt. Wyatt in turn had based his work on the recollections of his mother and an unnamed lady-in-waiting who both knew Anne Boleyn personally.

1. Brass of Sir Thomas Boleyn. (*Illustration from Charles Knight's* The Popular History of England, *1864*)

Nonetheless, current scholarship favours an earlier date of circa 1501 for her birth. Baron Herbert of Cherbury's biography of Henry VIII, published in 1649, was the first to suggest that Anne Boleyn was born around that time, perhaps even as early as 1498, though upon what authority Herbert did not say. It was not until 1981 that the case was properly made in support of Anne being born in 1501. The art historian Hugh Paget argued that as she went to the Low Countries in 1513, 1507 was implausible. Anne, he stated, was as a lady-in-waiting to the archduchess Margaret of Austria, and the acceptable age of service was 13 to 14. Therefore, Anne was certainly born earlier than when Camden and the others believed. But a re-examination of Paget's sources suggests that 1507 was closer to the truth as will later be addressed. Even if Anne Boleyn's birth date was properly determined, there is still the question of the relative ages of her siblings. While 1501 or 1507 have been proposed for Anne, it is not known when Mary and George were born, not to mention the late Thomas and Henry (or any other deceased children their parents may have had). Still, Mary is generally believed to have been the elder daughter as she would wed first, and George, perhaps somewhere in the middle between his sisters.

While Anne's age remains contentious, there is more agreement as to her birthplace. It was almost certainly at Blickling Hall in Norfolk; not its Jacobean incarnation as it is today, but the medieval manor house as acquired by Anne's great-grandfather Geoffrey Boleyn (or Bullen) in the middle of the fifteenth century. The tradition that Anne was born there was so well established by the 1760s, that a life-size bas relief sculpture of her likeness (albeit imaginary) was erected by the great staircase bearing the inscription *Anna Boleyn Hic Nata 1507* (*Anne Boleyn Was Born Here 1507*). Not only that, the bedroom in which she supposedly first drew breath was shown to the public until it was eventually demolished. Anne's imprint upon the house, along with that of the other Boleyns, was so strong that they inspired ghost stories. According to tradition, the spirit of a decapitated Anne would arrive at Blickling in a carriage drawn by phantom horses, as did a spectral Sir Thomas accompanied by a team of headless coachmen. Even his son George was said to make a haunting there. Within the house as the legends continue, was the creepy 'Old Bullen's Study'. Whatever was inside was supposedly so terrifying that the room was eventually bolted shut. Its location was subsequently forgotten.

As colourful as these tales are, Anne Boleyn and her family are better associated with Hever Castle. Nestled in the countryside of Kent in the village of Hever, near Edenbridge, the thirteenth-century property belonged to the Fiennes family until it fell into the ownership of Geoffrey Boleyn in 1462. By the time he was established in his new home, Boleyn

2. Blickling Hall in the Nineteenth Century. (*By James Baylis Allen after John Preston Neale*)

had done very well for himself. Born in 1406 to a family who may have had its origins in France, Geoffrey began his career as a mercer trading in hats. After the death of his first wife (a lady with the unusual name of Dionisia), he had made an advantageous marriage with Anne, the daughter of Thomas Hoo, First Baron Hoo and Hastings. By his early fifties, Boleyn had risen to be a sheriff of the city of London, and then a member of Parliament. His pinnacle of achievement was being elected Lord Mayor in 1457.

Geoffrey's son William and his four siblings were the first generation of Boleyns to be born at Blickling. Although he was a second son, William came into greater prominence because of a tragedy in the family. In 1471, his older brother Thomas died, and the 20-year-old William became their late father's heir, Geoffrey Boleyn having passed away eight years earlier. William inherited extensive properties and estates, including Blickling, and it was there that he and his Irish wife, Margaret Butler, daughter of the Seventh Earl of Ormond, started their family.

Having studied law for a time at Lincoln's Inn in the capital, William saw to it that his children, at least his sons, were also well educated. Thomas, born in about 1477, was especially bright. He was well read and had a talent for languages, excelling in Latin and French. His linguistic skills, coupled with his keen intelligence and his flair for negotiations, had Thomas on a path to royal service. His ancestors were no strangers to the crown. As far back as the Norman invasion of 1066, Eustace, the Count of Boulogne (from whom the Boleyns may well have been descended as the family name and its variants were English spellings of that French city) was in the entourage of William the Conqueror. Centuries later, Thomas's grandfather Geoffrey was known to both Henry VI and Edward IV. During the so-called War of the Roses fought between the families of Lancaster and York, he was called upon as London's mayor to keep the peace. Subsequently, his father William was knighted by Richard III at his crowning, and in the next reign, he rendered service to Henry VII, the first of the Tudors.

3. Coin of King Ferdinand and Queen Isabella of Spain.

In keeping up with his forebears, Thomas Boleyn aimed for a career at court. Like his father, he may have spent time at Lincoln's Inn, and perhaps have even studied at Cambridge University. By his own merits as a smart, hard-working, and likeable young man – and probably by a good word put in by his father – Thomas was in service to King Henry by 1501. That November, he witnessed his first great spectacle, the reception of the Princess of Spain in London. The arrival of Katherine of Aragon had long been in the making. Since she was a child, her parents, the rulers of a united Spain, Ferdinand of Aragon and Isabella of Castile, had been in talks with Henry VII for her marriage to his son Prince Arthur. In 1489, a treaty was made when Katherine was still only 3 and her fiancé slightly younger, but it was not until she was 15 that she finally found herself in England.

Katherine made her formal entry into London on 13 November. A pretty young lady with golden hair and a bright complexion, the princess was seated upon a mule and dressed in what the English considered a 'strange diversity of apparel'. By her side was the 10-year-old Prince Henry, soon to be her brother-in-law, explaining to Katherine in a mix

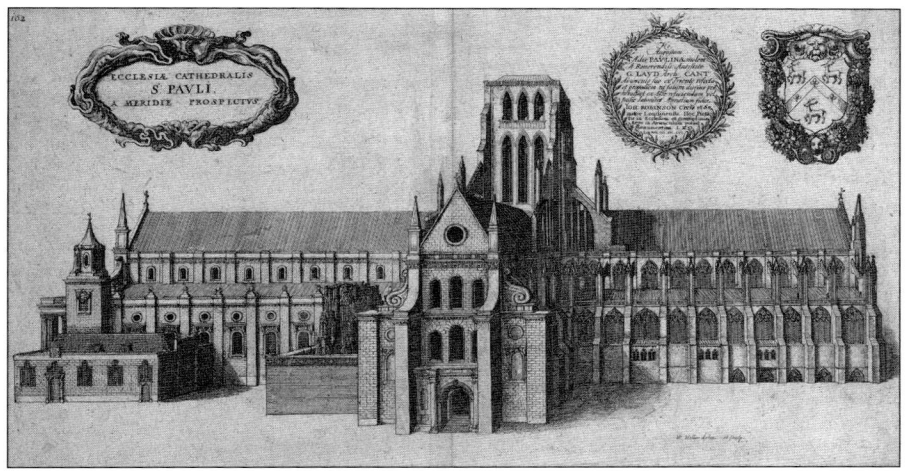

4. Saint Paul's Cathedral. (*By Wenceslaus Hollar*)

of Latin and French (she had yet to learn English), the meanings of the elaborate presentations staged before her in her honour.

Two days later, Thomas Boleyn was among those present at Saint Paul's Cathedral. The king's subjects had come by the thousands to see the young couple married. The number was 'so breme [great] and many, that in the rood lofts, vaults, windows, and on the pavements were to consider and behold nothing but visages'. Pressed against so many people, Thomas may have had trouble seeing Arthur and Katherine process up a long walkway to a platform erected before the high altar where they were made man and wife. Almost three decades later when so much was hinged upon that fateful day, Thomas would be called upon to testify as to what he remembered.

During his time at court, Thomas made enough of an impression to be given his first important assignment. In 1503, he was part of an escort – headed by the Earl of Surrey – taking the young Princess Margaret to Scotland where she was to wed King James IV. Thomas's association with Surrey actually went beyond their mission north together; the earl was in fact his father-in-law. His match to Elizabeth Howard was in accordance with the Boleyns' ambitions to better themselves by social climbing into the aristocracy. Surrey's father was John Howard, Duke of Norfolk, one of the greatest noblemen in the realm, and a descendent of King Edward I no less. Surrey should have inherited his father's title after he died fighting at the Battle of Bosworth in 1485, but for the fact that

8   Anne Boleyn

Norfolk had championed the wrong side. His allegiance to Richard III, who was also killed, proved an albatross to his family. The Howards were consequently out of favour with the new king, Henry VII. It would only be after years of loyal service – particularly at the Battle of Flodden Field where Surrey ironically fought and killed King James who had once welcomed him to Scotland – that the earl would finally be made Duke of Norfolk in 1514.

Thomas Boleyn and Elizabeth Howard's marriage was an arrangement decided by their families rather than a love match; the union of a courtier on the rise to a lady of great pedigree. It was a pact that benefitted both sides. But how the pair themselves felt about each other is a mystery. Neither one would leave any statements or writings about their relationship. The only certainty was that the couple were at least compatible enough to produce a good many children. Later it was believed that Elizabeth Howard did not long enjoy the pleasures of motherhood. According to the nineteenth-century biographer Agnes Strickland, Elizabeth passed away in 1512. But this was due to a misreading of a Boleyn genealogy, and in fact, Lady Boleyn would live on to survive two of her adult children.

While Thomas may have thought that his yearly income of £50 was inadequate to raise a family and to support a household, the Boleyns by all appearances lived a good and comfortable life. After all, the Earl of Surrey who had allowed Thomas to marry his daughter, obviously considered his son-in-law to be a young man of good prospects. Nothing is known of the specifics of how Thomas and Elizabeth brought up their three surviving children, but it was certain they had a conventional upbringing as the offspring of the well-to-do. From an early age, they were taught

5. Hever Castle in the Eighteenth Century. (*By Samuel and Nathaniel Buck*)

to obey their betters, beginning with their parents. Those in authority had to be shown their due respect, and this hierarchy extended up to the King of England, whose authority and right to rule was sanctioned by the Church.

The power and influence of religion in the Boleyns' daily lives could not be understated. Mary, Anne, and George were instructed in the tenets of the Christian faith and fully immersed in the Roman Catholic culture of early sixteenth-century England. Though some, such as the heretical Lollards, had dared to raise questions regarding the Faith and even sought corrections within the Church, the Boleyns – at least in their earlier years – were entirely conformist in their beliefs. God the Father – good and eternal – had formed the World into existence and gave breath to His greatest creation, humankind. But because of its failings, He then sent His son, Jesus Christ, to be offered up as sacrifice for its redemption.

That Christ could be made truly present through the consecration of bread and wine by a priest was a conviction that the Boleyn children were taught, and this great miracle was made evident to them at their regular attendance at Mass. As well, they were told that the pope in Rome, the apostolic successor to Saint Peter himself, was the greatest authority in Christendom and thus infallible. It was the duty of Anne and her siblings to live good lives and to look to the life everlasting following the passing of their earthly selves. The failure to do so would mean a prolonged stay in purgatory before reaching Heaven, or worse, the eternal damnation of one's soul to Hell.

To better achieve the glories of the hereafter, prayers were efficacious, especially if made on a daily basis as with a *Book of Hours* for example. Anne Boleyn herself owned such devotional works, and two are now kept at Hever Castle. Also, performing good deeds was considered essential for one's spiritual welfare, as were invocations made to the saints. Holy men and women were often prayed to for the outcome of affairs, from the important down to the mundane. Apart from the Mass, to actually be in the presence of the Divine was an experience many craved. Thousands flocked to sites associated with the saints or with the Virgin Mary Herself to worship, offer thanks, or ask for particular favours. Two of the most famous holy places in England were the tomb of the martyred Thomas Becket in Canterbury Cathedral and the Shrine of Walsingham in Norfolk. Later in life, even Anne would express a desire to visit the latter.

6. Christ in the Rosary. (*School of Dürer*)

Besides their religious education, Mary, Anne, and George were also instructed in more secular matters. They were taught to read and write, and some basic mathematics were included in their lessons; useful for men conducting business and for women put in charge of running a household. Drawing might also have been part of the curriculum devised by their tutors; an illustration of an armillary sphere by Anne appears in one of her *Book of Hours*. The social graces were not neglected. The children were taught how to conduct themselves properly, especially towards their superiors, and how to behave correctly at social gatherings. They were advised how to speak and dress well, and how to dance and play music. Dexterity on the lute and the virginals was particularly important. Many in the royal family became experts, and Anne herself was also acknowledged as being a skilled musician as an adult.

The children's world view was broadened by a study of literature, geography, and most essentially of languages. Some Latin was probably taught – enough for them to read from their prayer books and to follow the Mass with a missal – and certainly French. Thomas Boleyn was a proficient writer and speaker of it, and he was set on his children being likewise. It would seem that French lessons were given to his children beginning at a very young age. Early instruction in a foreign language was not unusual. In 1520, when she was only 4, Princess Mary, daughter of King Henry VIII (who succeeded his father in 1509), was able to receive a delegation of French envoys 'with most goodly countenance, [and] proper communication, and pleasant pastime in playing at the virginals', that 'they greatly marvelled and rejoiced the same, her young and tender age considered'.

Of the young Boleyns, it was Anne who emerged as the most precocious. She was already showing an aptitude for French, and Thomas saw an opportunity for her to be even better at it. Since 1512, he had been the English ambassador to the court of Margaret of Austria in the Netherlands. Thanks to his charm and informal manner, he had endeared himself to this remarkable lady. Although she had been born to greatness as the daughter of the Holy Roman Emperor Maximilian I, Margaret's life had not always been happy. When she was only 2, her mother, Mary of Burgundy, died after a riding accident. As a girl, Margaret was sent off to France to wed the future King Charles VIII, but he later repudiated her for another. A humiliated Margaret was then married to Prince John of Asturias, the son of Ferdinand and Isabella of

7. Margaret of Austria. (*By Bernard van Orley*)

Spain, only to have him pass away just six months afterwards. Their child, who might have been a consolation to the young widow, was tragically stillborn. Margaret's next match to Philibert II, Duke of Savoy, brought her contentment at last, but briefly. He died after three years. For Margaret there would be no more marriages, and for the rest of her life, she adopted mourning dress in memory of Philibert.

Still only 24, and having been 'too much unhappy in husbands', Margaret dedicated herself entirely to the interests of her family, the Hapsburgs. In 1507, she accepted the regency of the Netherlands,

8. Emperor Maximilian Receiving Margaret of Austria and His Grandchildren. (*By Hans Burgkmair*)

governing it in the name of nephew, Charles of Ghent (the future Holy Roman Emperor), who was still a minor. The boy's father, Philip of Castile (or Philip the Handsome as he was better known), had died the year before, and his mother, Joanna, daughter of the King and Queen of Spain, was incapacitated by insanity brought on by the death of her husband as it was given out.

Margaret proved to be a dedicated and capable governor, not to mention a concerned and loving guardian to her nephew and his three sisters: Eleanor (later Queen of Portugal and then of France), Isabeau (later Queen of Denmark, Norway, and Sweden), and Mary (later Queen of Hungary). She also gained the respect of her contemporaries who admired her for her knowledge and wisdom in political affairs and for her good nature. In spite of her past travails, Margaret retained a gracious demeanour and even a sense of humour. During a diplomatic meeting with the English in 1513 that included Charles Brandon, a favourite of King Henry VIII, she and the handsome courtier engaged in flirtatious banter that became the talk of the conference. But it was all a game, and Margaret, to her amusement, even allowed Brandon to purloin a ring right off her finger and to accept a bracelet from her as love tokens.

The regent was equally at ease with Thomas Boleyn. Though she was not coquettish as she was with Brandon, Margaret did show her sense of fun with him. On one occasion, she and Thomas put a bet – even shaking hands on it – on the outcome of a negotiation. If the matter was not settled to the satisfaction of the English within ten days, the archduchess must give Thomas her Spanish courser. But if it was, as Margaret thought it would be, he was obliged to surrender his small horse – a hobby – to her.

Having established such a good rapport with Margaret of Austria, Thomas sought a place for Anne at her court in the Netherlands. But why Anne instead of her presumably older sister Mary? Most likely because Thomas saw something in his second daughter that his first lacked. Perhaps Anne had a sharper intelligence and a better grasp of the rudimentary French that she was already learning at home. As well, being that Anne was still very young as it is proposed here, perhaps her youthfulness was better suited for the learning opportunities ahead.

In the early summer of 1513, Anne made ready for the Low Countries. She might have been accompanied by her parents, if so, only as far as Dover. Except for a female servant or two assigned to attend to her needs,

Anne was quite alone upon the ship sailing towards the Continent. What the feelings of such a little girl were on such a far-flung journey can only be imagined. Anne undoubtedly felt homesick already, but knowing of her later bold spirit, she might also have been excited at what life had in store for her beyond the sea.

Chapter 2

When Anne Boleyn landed on the Flemish coast, she and her party were met by Claude de Bouton, Lord of Corbaron, an envoy in the service of the Hapsburgs. Bouton brought her to Margaret of Austria, upon whom Anne made a very favourable impression. After assuring Thomas Boleyn by letter of his daughter's safe arrival, her new hostess could not help but add that she found Anne most intelligent and personable for her young years, and that she was indebted to him for placing the girl in her care. Margaret promised Thomas that she would do all she could for Anne – 'I am confident of being able to deal with her in a way which will give you satisfaction, so that on your return, the two of us will have no intermediary other than she.'

But what exactly did Margaret mean by her proper handling of Anne? It has been assumed that her sojourn in the Netherlands – apart from

9. The Court of Cambrai (the Keizershof) as it was in 1500. (*By August van den Eynde*)

improving her French – was for the privilege of being a lady-in-waiting to the regent. As her attendant, Anne would learn the social polish so important to her father. Because the archduchess supposedly insisted that girls be of the right age (that is about 13 or 14) to enter her service, Anne must have been born in 1501 as Hugh Paget opined. Paget referred to a letter written in 1512 by Emperor Maximilian to Margaret in which he asked her to place the niece of the Spanish courtier and ambassador, Don Diégo de Guevara, with his 'most dear and most loved' granddaughters in the city of Mechelen (Malines). The three princesses were about the same age as Don Diégo's niece. The emperor was loathe to deny this request as he had promised the envoy long ago that when the girl attained the age of between 13 to 14, she could come to court.

10. Don Diégo de Guevara(?). (*By Michel Sittow*)

But it is not certain that the purpose was for her to be a maid-of-honour. As Maximilian was specific that she was to join the Hapsburg young ladies, the intention may have been for Don Diégo's niece to act as a companion to them and to finish her education with the emperor's granddaughters. That said, instead of boarding with Margaret of Austria at her palace called the Court of Savoy, she was probably housed with the Imperial children at the old palace of Margaret of York (the step-grandmother of the archduchess) known as the Court of Cambrai, or Keizershof, which was directly across the street. The young woman's coming to Mechelen may also well have been to find herself a good match. And as for her being of the right age, this might rather have been something formerly stipulated by her own family, rather than by the Hapsburgs.

That Anne Boleyn may likewise not have performed the duties of a lady-in-waiting to Margaret of Austria is implied in a letter of hers. Upon her arrival in the Netherlands, she was packed off to the Imperial

Part I   17

retreat at Castle Tervuren in La Veure in Brabant where the regent liked to spend her spring and summer holidays with her charges. Anne must have been dazzled by her first sight of the Hapsburg castle, which was like nothing she had ever seen in her native Norfolk and Kent, or on her way to Dover. The palace consisted of a series of grand multi-storey interconnected buildings of white stone surrounded by a lake. Beyond it were lovely gardens to wander through and parklands filled with wild game for the chase. It was from this beautiful fairytale-like castle that Anne began her education, rather than service to the archduchess as often thought.

From Castle Tervuren, Anne wrote a series of dispatches to Thomas Boleyn. She had been given a tutor named Semmonet who would compose and dictate letters which his English pupil would then write out in French as best she could. Unfortunately, none of these has survived except for one which Anne wrote herself without Semmonet's assistance. In this letter to her father, she expressed her gratitude for being sent abroad, and she assured him that she would always be a devoted daughter. Anne also promised to 'continue to learn to speak good French', as 'the queen will

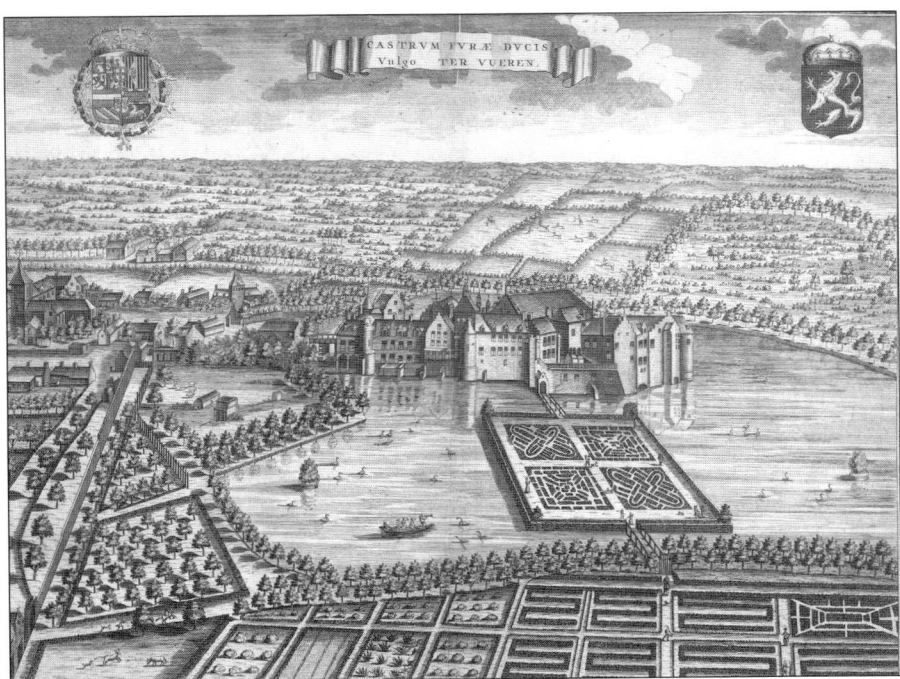

11. Castle Tervuren in La Veure. (*From Antonius Sanderus's* Chorographia Sacra Brabantiae)

take the trouble to speak to me, and I am greatly looking forward to the prospect of talking with a person so wise and honourable'.

But who exactly was 'the queen' Anne was referring to – Katherine of Aragon (now the wife of Henry VIII) or Margaret of Austria? If the former, then Thomas Boleyn was already mapping out Anne's future. She would receive her education with the regent and when the time came, she would go home where she would be received by the Queen of England, who would hopefully employ her in the royal household. But why would the Spanish-born Katherine wish to converse with Anne in French? Despite the belief that she had a 'meagre knowledge' of it, the queen actually spoke French very well; it was probably better than her English. In the summer of 1498, the Spanish ambassador had told Queen Isabella that Elizabeth of York, the wife of King Henry VII, and her mother-in-law, the Countess of Richmond, wished

> that the Princess of Wales should always speak French with the Princess Margaret, who is now in Spain, in order to learn the language, and to be able to converse in it when she comes to England. This is necessary, because these ladies do not understand Latin, and much less Spanish.

By the time she arrived in England, Katherine – after three years of instruction by Margaret of Austria – was reported to be making good progress at it to the delight of Queen Elizabeth. As for her English, Katherine would have only started to learn it after she became Prince Arthur's wife.

But if it was not Katherine of Aragon Anne had been referring to, it was undoubtedly Margaret of Austria, whom she had mistakenly called 'the queen', rather than 'the regent' or 'the governor'. Taking the archduchess into consideration, Anne's letter inferred that she actually had little interaction with Margaret at first. As she herself stated that she had already written a number of letters to Thomas Boleyn, this implied that some time – probably weeks – had passed since her arrival in the Low Countries. If that was the case, Anne had yet to properly converse with the archduchess. Except for when Bouton introduced her to Margaret – probably just a brief welcome and an exchange of pleasantries – Anne appeared to have had meagre contact with the great lady. From a letter written by Margaret to her father Maximilian, it appeared that she herself was not at La Veure in the spring and summer of 1513, or if she was, only briefly. She told the emperor how his teenage grandson Charles who had gone there, had accidently shot and killed a local man with a crossbow at the end of May. The archduchess appeared to be westward at the time as she was expecting a delegation of Danes come to negotiate the marriage of her niece Isabeau. They had just arrived in Antwerp, and the regent was most probably waiting for them in Brussels where she normally conducted affairs of state in the spring and summer. If Margaret was in Brussels, Anne may have met her there momentarily when she arrived in the Netherlands, and she was then sent off to Castle Tervuren in La Veure. There Anne began her French lessons, and as she wrote Thomas Boleyn, when she was to go to court in the autumn– meaning that of the Savoy in Mechelen – she hoped to properly converse with her hostess.

12. The Arrival of the Statue of Notre Dame du Sablon in Brussels, detail. (*By Bernard van Orley*) On the left of the tapestry, Charles of Ghent and his brother Ferdinand are seen carrying the cult statue. On the right, Margaret of Austria is at worship before it, accompanied by her nephew Ferdinand and her nieces Eleanor, Isabeau, Mary, and Catherine. In reality, Catherine did not live with Margaret, but was raised in Spain.

Because Anne was likely intended for the schoolroom, she would not have served the archduchess as a round-the-clock maid-of-honour. Instead, she may have attended upon Margaret of Austria on occasion as to learn courtly etiquette. Still, Hugh Paget was certain that Anne was fully engaged as a lady-in-waiting as she was supposedly included in a register of Margaret's servants; among the eighteen women in her company was one named 'Bullan'. However, this list was actually compiled in April 1525, part of a household ordinance created by the regent herself. By that time, Anne had long left the Netherlands. Furthermore, 'Bullan' is a misreading. The lady in question was actually Mademoiselle de Bulleux, most likely the daughter or relative of Hugues de Bulleux, Chatelaine of the Château d'Aïre, Lord of Franqueville, and Lord Chamberlain to Margaret.

That a very young Anne Boleyn – born in 1507 – was most probably in the Imperial schoolroom was put forward by the historian Retha Warnicke. She had pointed out the example of the 7-year-old daughter of Charles Brandon, to whom Margaret of Austria had played hostess to as well. Additionally, the regent had extended an invitation to Brandon's ward, Magdalen Rochester, a girl of 8. They had come to be educated, along with other children boarding at Margaret's court. These *enfants d'honneur* – as recently pointed out – were the offspring of the great and wealthy given a place with the regent to learn alongside her nephew and nieces. Anne, as the daughter of an ambassador, would have been allowed

13. Mechelen. (*By Georg Braun and Franz Hogenberg in* Civitates orbis terrarum)

into this elite group too. At the time of her stay with the archduchess, there were about twenty other children – originating from the Imperial territories and beyond – in residence as well. Their presence suggests that Anne was as youthful as they were, as does Margaret's statement that Anne was 'bright and pleasant for her young age'. Also, it was not insignificant that in August 1514, Thomas Boleyn called her 'my daughter the little Boleyn'.

* * *

With the arrival of autumn, Margaret of Austria packed up the children at La Veure and returned north to Mechelen. One of the finest cities of the Habsburg Netherlands, the Seigniory of Mechelen was a great and prosperous commercial centre when the archduchess assumed her regency. It was renowned for its fine cloth (especially its linen), and it was also recognized for its skilled craftsmanship in leatherwork, metalsmithing, and painting. Besides its importance to trade, Mechelen in itself was a most handsome city. It was encircled by the River Dyle which also 'passed through the town and made a number of small islands in the town, both to the great ornament and commodity thereof'. Yet Mechelen was subject to flooding, and it was purposely built as a 'goodly strong town' to withstand rising waters. The city boasted a number of fine churches. In the centre by the market square, was Saint Rumbold's

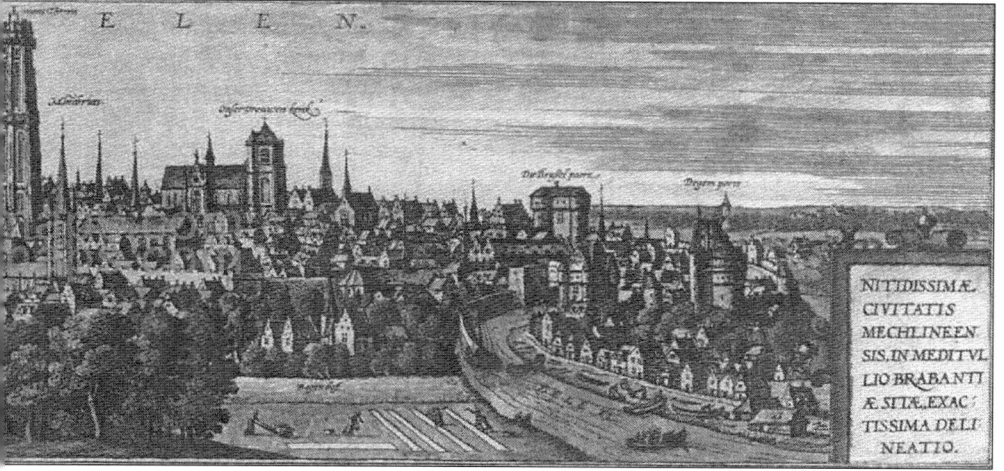

Cathedral with its great tower that could be seen from miles away. To the east, there was the Church of Saint Peter next to Margaret of Austria's palace. The archduchess usually worshipped in her private chapel within the Savoy, but if she wished to attend public services, she had use of a walkway leading to an oratory in Saint Peter's.

Margaret's showplace was her palace, the Court of Savoy. After she was appointed regent, the archduchess expanded the building as it was too small to be an effective powerbase for her and her family. Nearby properties were acquired which were then transformed for Margaret's use. The project was so ambitious that she would actually not live to see its completion. When Anne Boleyn arrived at the Savoy in the autumn of 1513, she would have seen the work still in progress. The palace was conceived as a Renaissance-style, four-sided complex built around an open-air inner courtyard. While the northern stretch had still yet to be started, what had been done so far would have impressed Anne. Parts of the medieval houses belonging to Margaret of York were incorporated into the archduchess's new headquarters as the west wing. Her private rooms were on the ground floor with windows looking out towards the courtyard, probably planted with trees and scented by flowers at the time. Even more imposing was the Savoy's southern range. It was built of reddish-brown brick with an open arcade on the bottom floor with arches rising from columns on its façade. Directly above, the first level offered views of the quad from a balcony, while the second storey was contained under a great roof with dormer windows providing light to the interior. Margaret was such an enthusiastic builder that she also commissioned the construction of a church – the Royal Monastery of Brou – in which she ordered the making of her tomb.

Being a lady of culture and sophistication, this 'most redoubtable' lady as Thomas Boleyn called her, Margaret of Austria fashioned one of the most extravagant courts in Europe at the Savoy. In emulation of her ancestors, the Dukes of Burgundy, the archduchess welcomed artists and men of letters to Mechelen. The walls of her palace were covered by rich tapestries and adorned with paintings by artists such as Jan Gossaert (Mabuse), a prolific artist of the Dutch Renaissance, Hieronymus Bosch, known for his pictures of the strange and otherworldly, and Jan van Eyck, court painter to her great-grandfather Philip the Good. The archduchess, cognizant of her great lineage, was also fond of collecting portraits of her

Part I 23

14. The Court of Savoy in the Nineteenth Century. (*By Jan Baptist De Noter*)

family. Her private rooms and the more public space of her library were decorated with pictures of her Burgundian predecessors on her mother's side, as well as the Hapsburgs on her father's. There were also images of foreign royals associated with Margaret. As Anne Boleyn was a guest of the archduchess, she may have been permitted to view these portraits, and interestingly, come to know two of the sitters intimately in the future: Katherine of Aragon and her sister-in-law Mary Tudor.

Besides painters, Margaret also patronized illuminators of manuscripts and books, such as the Horenbouts (or Horneboltes). Gerard, the head of the family, would later be appointed as her court painter in 1515, while his children Lucas and Susanna learnt the family business from their father. But by the mid-1520s, the Horenbouts were in England in royal service. It has been suggested that their emigration was through the agency of Thomas Boleyn, who as ambassador might have come to know the family and encouraged them to settle in his native country.

Illuminations, such as those done by the Horenbouts, were not only found in religious texts or in volumes of literature in Margaret's court, but also in song books as decoration. The archduchess had a great love of music, and she had amassed a sizeable collection of works by her favourite composers, some of whom she lent her patronage. Anne Boleyn appeared to have shared Margaret's tastes. Later in life, she would come

15. Emperor Maximilian from the Choirbook of Margaret of Austria. (*Attributed to Gerard Horenbout*)

in possession of a music book which contained motets and chansons by composers known to the archduchess.

Margaret's collecting went beyond just pictures and books. Her inventories also list jewellery, sculptures, scientific instruments, liturgical items, and even amusements such as table-top games. The regent was especially interested in curios, chiefly specimens of nature. For instance, she was very fond of coral, both in its natural state and carved. But most interesting was Margaret's assortment of exotica from the New World, which Anne Boleyn may have been privileged to see. During her brief marriage to Prince John of Spain in 1497, Christopher Columbus had already made two voyages across the ocean. Years afterwards, when Margaret had set herself up in Mechelen, some of the artifacts brought back from Columbus's explorations of the so-called 'Indies' could be found in her chambers at the Savoy. The regent also had an extensive collection of maps, which Anne may also have seen. These incorporated the latest information of what was known of the world at large, including the latest discoveries across the Atlantic. In perusing these charts, Anne must have been enthralled by what lay beyond the confines of Europe.

As she was probably in the Imperial schoolroom, Anne was most likely living at the Court of Cambrai, rather than at the Savoy. Her companions would have been the regent's three nieces – Cambrai being divided into two households, one for Charles of Ghent and the other for his sisters – with whom she may have shared lessons or at least with the youngest, Mary of Austria, born in 1505. However, nothing is known of how the Hapsburg siblings interacted with Anne or what they thought of this girl from a faraway country with her strange language and customs. Only when Anne achieved her later notoriety were their opinions of her set down. Mary, as the widowed Queen of Hungary and then Governor of the Netherlands, would call her *méchante* (evil). But that was far in the future, and at the time Anne took her place with the Imperial princesses, there is no reason to believe that they did not find her as amiable as their aunt did.

Anne celebrated Christmas with the Hapsburgs, as well as the other great religious holidays. On Shrove Tuesday 1514, before the solemn season of Easter was to begin, Margaret of Austria and her court went to the great market by Saint Rumbold's to watch the tournaments and to enjoy the offerings of food laid out for her and the Imperial children. Anne would no doubt have been invited to come along, and also to the traditional Ascension Day deer hunt in which Charles of Ghent took part. Anne would have kept company with his sisters as they all watched from a tavern by the cathedral.

Later that spring, Anne went on vacation with the Imperial family. As the archduchess wrote to her father that May, 'to give pleasure to Monsieur my nephew and to Mesdames my nieces' she was going to take them to La Veure again for a treat. However, the stay was short. Even though summer was approaching and Margaret had closed up the Court of Savoy, she could not afford to be idle for long as she had affairs to attend to in Brussels. Usually, Margaret left the children at Castle Tervuren, but their presence was required in the city for a great occasion.

In early June, Margaret and her family were in Brussels at the Palace of Coudenberg. Anne, who most likely had joined them, observed the marriage by proxy of the 12-year-old Madame Isabeau to King Christian II of Denmark and Norway (and later Sweden) on the 11th, held in the great

16. The Coudenberg Palace. (*By Jan van de Velde*)

hall named the Aula Magna. Before witnesses, the princess made her vows with the Danish ambassador standing in for his master. Following the Nuptial Mass, a feast was held along with tournaments outside. At night, the wedding was further solemnized by the ritual bedding of Isabeau and the envoy. The two laid down together for a moment, and the union was declared consummated. For all its grandeur and celebration, the young bride herself might have been apprehensive of what was to come. Her new husband at 33 was much older than she, and Isabeau may have heard that King Christian, despite his new commitment, was insistent on keeping his mistress to whom he was devoted to. Anne might have come to sympathize with Isabeau. Later, she would find herself in similar circumstances – promised to a man she did not know or love, but was obliged to have him all the same.

In the months since her arrival in the Netherlands, Anne's French had improved immensely, and she was speaking it with ease. So much that in 1514, a special request for her was made by none other than Mary Tudor, the sister of the King of England. As it was the duty of many a princess to form a marital alliance, the 18-year-old Mary was to wed the King of France, Louis XII. That he was her senior by thirty-four years made no difference to her brother Henry VIII or to his chief minister, Cardinal Thomas Wolsey, who both wanted a treaty with France. Interestingly, Mary was originally intended elsewhere, to none other than Margaret of Austria's nephew Charles of Ghent, which explains why her portrait had been so prominently displayed at the regent's palace. Despite the notes of affection and love tokens that the young couple – she was 11 and he was 7 at the time – had sent each other as they were expected to, the marriage never took place. Relations between England and the empire had soured, and France was now deemed a better prospect to Henry VIII. Instead of taking a husband younger than herself, Mary would now wed one significantly older.

Louis could not have been appealing to such a young woman, but Mary played her part as she must. In response to the French king's love letters, she wrote sweet nothings back to him, saying for example how 'there is nothing more that I desire than to see you'. Still, Louis was old by the standards of his time, and there was talk that he was not at all well. With an eye to her future and that she was already in love with Charles Brandon, now Duke of Suffolk, Mary extracted a promise from

17. Altarpiece with Christian II and Isabeau of Austria. (*By an Unknown Artist*)

her brother Henry VIII that 'if I should fortune to survive the said king, I might with your good will, marry myself at my liberty without your displeasure'.

Mary Tudor's upcoming marriage would alter the course of Anne Boleyn's life. It can be imagined that her time with Margaret of Austria would have been a longer one, and with her excellent French and her fine deportment learnt at the archduchess's court, Anne might well have made a good marriage for herself in the Netherlands. However, she was still an English subject and her father's daughter, and her fate was out of her own hands. In preparation for her journey to France, Mary Tudor had need of attendants. Already, Anne's sibling Mary Boleyn had been selected to wait upon the princess, and Anne's presence was needed as well. Her sister Mary had undoubtedly been chosen as she knew French, and owing to a lack of other fluent speakers, it was natural that that the princess would want Anne in her train too, despite her young age. Even though Mary Tudor herself spoke French since she was a child, it was essential that her servants did likewise to function effectively at King Louis' court. Anne's principal duty was probably to act as an interpreter for those in Mary's staff – numbering about 150 – who could only speak English, and to join her new mistress in her interactions with her French subjects.

18. Medal of Louis XII. (*By an Unknown Artist*)

The demand for Anne put Thomas Boleyn – who had likewise been ordered to accompany the king's sister to France – in an awkward position. It was he who had asked Margaret of Austria to accept his daughter in the first place, and now he had to ask for her return. As well, the archduchess would hardly be pleased that an English princess – once meant for her nephew Charles – was now allied to a family unfriendly to her own. And to add insult to injury, she would have to surrender Anne to the country in which she herself had been rejected by in her youth twenty-three years ago. Still, Thomas could not disobey a royal command seeking Anne, and on 14 August, he wrote to the regent:

The sister of the king my master, Madame Mary, betrothed as Queen of France, wants to have with her my daughter the little Boleyn, whom my most redoubtable lady has with her presently at her court. To this request, I cannot at all refuse.

Nor could Margaret. As fond as she had become of Anne, and as distasteful as the marriage was to her, she could not reasonably object. She allowed the girl to leave for France to whatever destiny had in store for her.

Chapter 3

On the morning of Sunday, 5 November 1514, a great crowd gathered in the Basilica of Saint Denis outside of Paris. It had come to witness a glittering and sacred event, the crowning of the king's new wife. Less than a month ago, Mary Tudor was married to Louis XII, and in recognition of her as his queen and as an expression of his love for her, he was now honouring her with a coronation.

At the appointed hour, Mary, escorted by Francis of Valois, Duke of Brittany, a cousin of the king and his heir until he had a son – Louis' three boys by his late wife Queen Anne had all died young – arrived at the church with 'a great company of noblemen and ladies'. Included among them were Anne and Mary Boleyn acting as Mary's attendants. They were all led into Saint Denis' vast interior by an assemblage of French

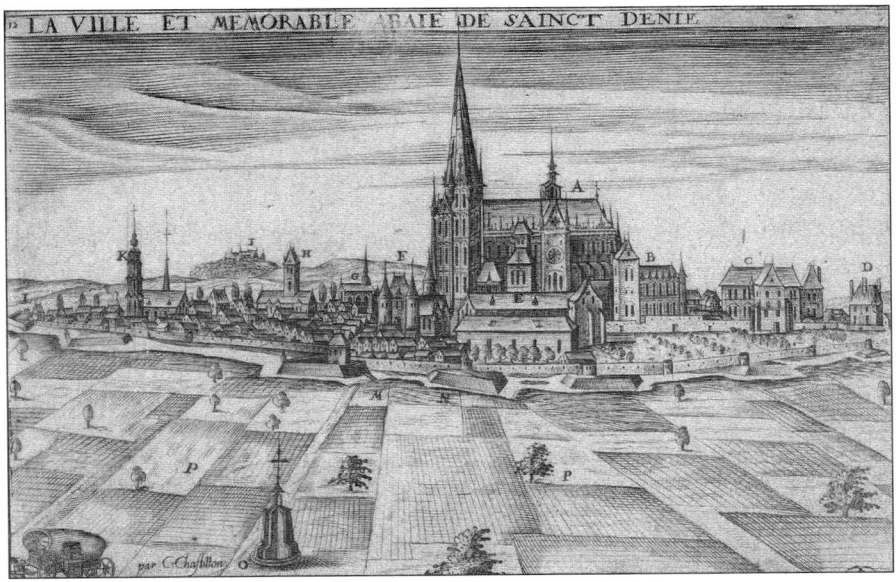

19. The City and Memorable Abbey of Saint Denis. (By *Claude Chastillon in* Topographie françoise)

aristocrats. Their number was so many that the English ambassadors invited to the ceremony, which included the Duke of Suffolk, lost count of them.

The new queen consort was brought before the high altar where she knelt for the ancient rituals to confirm her title. Mary was anointed with holy oil, and a ring was slipped onto her finger signifying her as the king's wife. As she remained on her knees, two sceptres were placed into her hands, and finally, the crown set upon her head. For the Coronation Mass that followed, Mary was seated in a chair set upon the left side of the altar. During the service, she conducted herself with the utmost dignity, but it was noticed that the heavy weight of the crown gave her much discomfort. It was removed, and Duke Francis, who was standing nearby, held it above her head instead as the Mass continued. From her place, Mary could observe the consecrations without distraction, and if she looked straight ahead, she could see Charles Brandon watching her from the choir directly opposite. Despite the solemnity of the occasion, it can be supposed that the two could not help but exchange meaningful glances with each other.

On the next day, Mary made her grand entry into Paris as the crowned and anointed Queen of France. She set out from the outskirts of Saint Denis where the city officials, joined by clergyman – said to number 3,000 – greeted her. Mary was resplendent in her litter covered in white cloth-of-gold and drawn by horses draped in gold as well. With her pale skin, delicate features, and golden-brown hair, Mary was famed for her beauty – she was even called 'a paradise' – and she looked even more magnificent wearing an abundance of jewels, which included 'a coronall [crown] of great pearls', given to her by her adoring husband. On the way to Paris, the new queen was joined by a company that included Francis of Valois and the Duke of Suffolk. A stop was made at the Cathedral of Notre Dame where Mary, to demonstrate her piety, left an offering. She then proceeded to the royal palace where King Louis waited for her. There, a banquet was held to further celebrate the queen's arrival in the city, and before the night was over, there was much 'dancing and pastime' at which the Boleyn sisters would have joined in.

Mary Boleyn was probably lodged with the other ladies-in-waiting at the palace, but Anne, due to her younger years, was likely placed with the 4-year-old Princess Renée at the Château de Vincennes not far away.

20. Paris. (*By Léonard Gaultier*)

Surrounded by forest, the fortress was originally built as a hunting lodge in the twelfth century. It was subsequently enlarged with a central keep built within, along with a chapel and quarters for the royal family. A moat was also added for defence if needed. The château served as the residence of Renée, the younger daughter of King Louis by his first wife. In no time, a warm friendship developed between Renée and Anne. Many years later as the widowed Duchess of Ferrara, Renée would tell an English diplomat that she especially 'loved and honoured' his mistress Elizabeth I because 'the queen her mother and myself were old friends together'. The closeness of the two girls suggests they were not far apart in age, giving further reason to believe that Anne was born in 1507 rather than earlier.

As much as Renée and her elder sister Claude were adored by their father, neither of them could be Queen Regnant of France. Under French law, a woman could not succeed to the crown, and thus Louis XII still had no direct heir. But with his marriage to Mary Tudor, it was hoped that she would correct this deficiency. Mary had come from good stock. Her mother, Elizabeth of York, had seven children – though four of them died young – and there was no reason to think that Mary could not fulfil her duty too. She was young and healthy, and Louis, despite his years, was presumably still virile.

But a *dauphin* – his longed-for successor – remained an unfulfilled wish for Louis. On the evening of 1 January 1515, the old king died. It was said that in his enthusiasm to father a son, he was worn out in bed by the queen. Louis had so loved his wife that

21. Renée of France. (*From* Guillaume Rouillé's La seconde partie du proptuaire de medalles, *1577*)

> he gave himself over to behold too much her excellent beauty, being then but 18 years of age, nothing considering the proportion of his own years, nor his decayed complexion, so that he fell into the rage of a fever, which drawing to it a sudden flux, overcame in one instant [his] life.

An illness – not sexual overexertion – was more likely the cause of the king's death, but whatever the case, Mary was put into a bleak position. She was no longer Queen of France and she was without friends in a foreign land. Even months ago, when she first arrived in her new country, she was already upset by Louis' abrupt dismissal of some of her English staff. Those that remained with her, Mary complained, 'never had experience, nor knowledge how to advise or give me counsel in any time of need.' While the queen had never specifically mentioned Mary Boleyn (or her sister Anne, had she already joined her service), such young ladies had been of no help to her before, and they were still in no position to do anything for her now. In place of sound advice as to what their mistress ought to do next, all they could do was to offer her their sympathies as a widow. As well, they saw to it that Mary was made as comfortable as possible as she withdrew from court and assumed the *deuil blanc*, the traditional white dress of mourning in France. For forty days, Mary and her women shut themselves in darkened rooms with curtains drawn in bereavement for the king. As they cared for their mistress, her servants were to expressly notice any signs of pregnancy. A posthumous child of Louis' would inherit the realm, and so displace the claim of his cousin, Francis of Valois. Needless to say, he was desperately hoping that Mary was without child. In February, when she finally emerged from her seclusion with no such symptoms, Francis breathed a sigh of relief. Even though he had already been crowned king on 25 January, a son of Louis and Mary would challenge his claim to the throne.

Mindful of her future, Mary had no desire to be used again as her brother's pawn in the royal marriage market. Though she had banished Charles Brandon from her mind and had set herself to be a good wife to

22. Mary, Queen of France and Charles Brandon, Duke of Suffolk. (*By George Vertue after an Unknown Artist*)

King Louis, her new situation gave her the opportunity to consider the duke once again. Mary had always been in love with Suffolk, and she was determined to seek personal happiness by being with him. After Charles arrived in Paris – his mission to take her home as he had promised her brother Henry VIII – he was confronted by a desperate Mary who demanded that he either marry her right there and then or never at all. 'I never saw woman so weep,' the duke later said, and overcome by chivalry and love, he made her his wife in a secret ceremony. Henry was incensed as expected; so much that Suffolk, despite his deep friendship with the king, feared the loss of his head should he and his new bride go back home. Eventually, Henry's temper cooled. He still had too much affection for his sister and his new brother-in law, and with the couple's agreement to a hefty fine – a sum of £24,000 (close to £16 million today), the repayment of Mary's dowry, and the surrender of her French jewels – they were allowed to return to England and be back in Henry's good graces.

Whether Anne was at court or at Vincennes when at this drama unfolded is unknown. She would either have learnt the details directly or through gossip – so sensational was this story of the former queen who

23. The Castle Royal in the Forest of Vincennes. (*By an Unknown Artist*)

defied her mighty brother to follow the dictates of her heart. Anne might well have admired Mary Tudor's boldness and was inspired by it. In a time when women's futures were dictated by men, it was still possible to make one's own way in the world, and even find happiness along the way. As such, Anne may have seen Mary as a role model, that is at least until circumstances to come pitted them against each other.

With the departure of the 'French Queen' (as Mary Tudor continued to be referred to as), her household was disbanded. Her English servants, including Mary Boleyn, set sail with her and Charles Brandon. However, Anne was left behind. This was not due to unkindness on the part of the new Duchess of Suffolk, but because her stepdaughter and successor, Claude, asked that Anne remain. This may well have had to do with her bilingualism as Claude herself could only speak French, and as the new queen, she would be expected to welcome English visitors to her court and an interpreter would be needed at times. Apart from Anne's value as an intermediary, it could also have been that Claude, like her sister Renée, had taken a liking to her.

The eldest daughter of Louis XII and Anne of Brittany, Claude had been married to Francis of Valois since 1514. As the new Queen of France, Claude drew unfavourable comparisons to her former mother-in-law. Unlike the vivacious and lovely Mary, she was of a reserved and retiring disposition, and thus preferred a quiet life at court. Perhaps Claude was especially self-conscious. Prior to her marriage, Pierre de Rohan, the Marshal of France and tutor to Francis as a boy, had voiced his concern that the princess would be unable to have offspring because she was 'malformed in person'. As such, he would rather Francis marry 'the most insignificant shepherdess in the kingdom', Rohan said unkindly, than Princess Claude. The marshal was wrong, and Claude went on to provide her husband with children – seven in fact – though her health would suffer accordingly.

While Claude was content to stay in the background, her husband Francis basked in the spotlight as king. He was as flamboyant as the gorgeous clothes and jewels he wore, and he was determined to create a court that would be the most celebrated in all of Christendom. Brought up by his mother, the formidable Louise of Savoy, who instilled a love of the ideals and culture of the Renaissance upon him and his sister Margaret, the new king looked to Italy for inspiration. He invited its artists into his service, including the venerable Leonardo da Vinci, to whom he offered a house and a pension; might Anne Boleyn have seen him at court? Francis was a great aficionado of da Vinci's work – he later acquired his famed *La Gioconda* (or *Mona Lisa*) – and he became personally fond of the old man as well. Tradition had it that when da Vinci died in 1519, it was in the arms of a grieving Francis. The king's interest in the Renaissance also extended to his building projects. The Château de Chambord in the Loire Valley was possibly designed by another Italian, Domenico da Cortona, or as it has been postulated, by da Vinci himself. Literature had a place at Francis's court too. His brilliant sister, Margaret of Angoulême, held salons attended by writers and poets, and she herself would be known as a respected author. Among her works were poetical compositions, both secular and religious, and even a collection of stories called the *Heptameron*.

The *Heptameron*'s tales of love and sex would have been ideal reading for the lascivious King of France. Francis had a reputation as a ladies' man.

24. Queen Claude. (*By an Unknown Artist*)

25. Francis I. (*Workshop of Joos Van Cleve*)

While he revelled in displays of athletic prowess and in pursuits of martial glory with his male friends, it was really the company of woman that he preferred. 'A court without women,' Francis said, 'is like a year without a spring, like a spring without roses.' Among his conquests were Mary Boleyn when she was in the service of the former queen, and more recently, Françoise de Foix, Countess of Châteaubriant. Though Francis never flaunted his affairs in front of Claude – he was always kind and respectful to the mother of his children – his extramarital affairs were no secret at court. Francis himself boasted about them, even if it meant being crass and ruining the reputations of those he had slept with. Of Mistress Boleyn, he had choice words demeaning her as 'a great prostitute and infamous above all'. In spite of her husband's infidelities, Claude made no scenes. She turned a blind eye and discouraged her maids from the excesses of Francis's court. As the years passed, the queen might have become uneasy when her randy spouse began noticing the maturing dark-haired Anne Boleyn. He even wrote verses in tribute to her:

> *Venus was blonde, I've been told,*
> *Now I see she's a brunette.*

Under Claude's watchful eye, Anne Boleyn continued with her education while serving the queen as a *demoiselle d'honneur* at the same time. Anne's ability to understand both English and French would be an asset to Claude for the great summit to be held in June 1520 between her husband and Henry VIII. While the King of England and his Spanish wife both spoke French fluently, others in their suite did not. Anne could be put to good use as an interpreter. When she was told that she would be coming along, Anne must have been excited for the opportunity to be present at such an important event and to be asked to put her talents to use. As well, she would get to see her parents and siblings – all in attendance upon King Henry and Queen Katherine – again after years apart from them.

The purpose of the gathering was to confirm the new Anglo-French alliance, one to be sealed by a marriage between the 4-year-old Princess Mary of England and the *dauphin* of France (Francis's son born in 1518). Ever since Henry and Francis came to their respective crowns, there had been a tension between them. This would suggest that they were

26. Henry VIII. (*By Cornelis Anthonisz*)

opposites; but on the contrary, the two kings were much alike. They were close in age – only three years apart – and both were determined to make their mark on the international stage, even if it meant trumping the other in politics, and in war if necessary. Their rivalry was even personal. In 1515, when the Venetian envoy, Sebastiano Giustiniani, visited the English court, Henry VIII peppered him with questions about Francis whom he had yet to meet. 'Talk with me awhile!' Henry said heartily. 'The King of France, is he as tall as I am?' There was 'but little difference,' the ambassador replied. At over six feet tall, Henry was put off that Francis was about the same. Wanting to best the French king, he then asked if he was 'as stout'. Francis was not as strongly made, Giustiniani admitted. Pleased at last, Henry pressed on. 'What sort of legs has he?' he inquired. 'Spare' was the answer. Satisfied at last that he was the better man than Francis, Henry opened up his doublet and cried, 'Look here! And I have also a good calf to my leg!'

In preparation for the summit, a valley (the 'Vale of Gold') between Ardres situated in French territory and Guînes (Guisnes) located in the English-held Pale of Calais was selected as the appropriate meeting place. There, large tents were erected, all covered in rich fabrics which caught the light of the sun. The abundance of golden cloth would earn the event the name of *Le Champ de Drap d'or*, or as the English called it, *The Field of the Cloth-of-Gold*. There were also more practical considerations of course. As the summit was expected to run over three weeks, provisions were needed to feed the multitudes from both sides. The royal purveyors made sure an ample supply of food and drink was in readiness, along with herds of livestock ready for slaughter. For cooking, huge kitchens were constructed on the spot, complete with large open-air ovens.

Henry VIII also sent a team of workmen – surveyors, architects, carpenters, and artisans – to provide lodgings for himself. No expense had been spared to dazzle the French. A two-storey mansion was erected in Guînes from scratch made of timber, canvas, and brick. In front was a great arched entryway decorated with festoons, Tudor roses of red and white, and the royal arms of England, while on top, the roof was graced with statuary. The interior was just as impressive. There were spacious quarters for Henry and Katherine, and there were even rooms for his Lord Chancellor Cardinal Wolsey, and for the Duke of Suffolk and the former Queen of France, who were to come as well. In addition, there

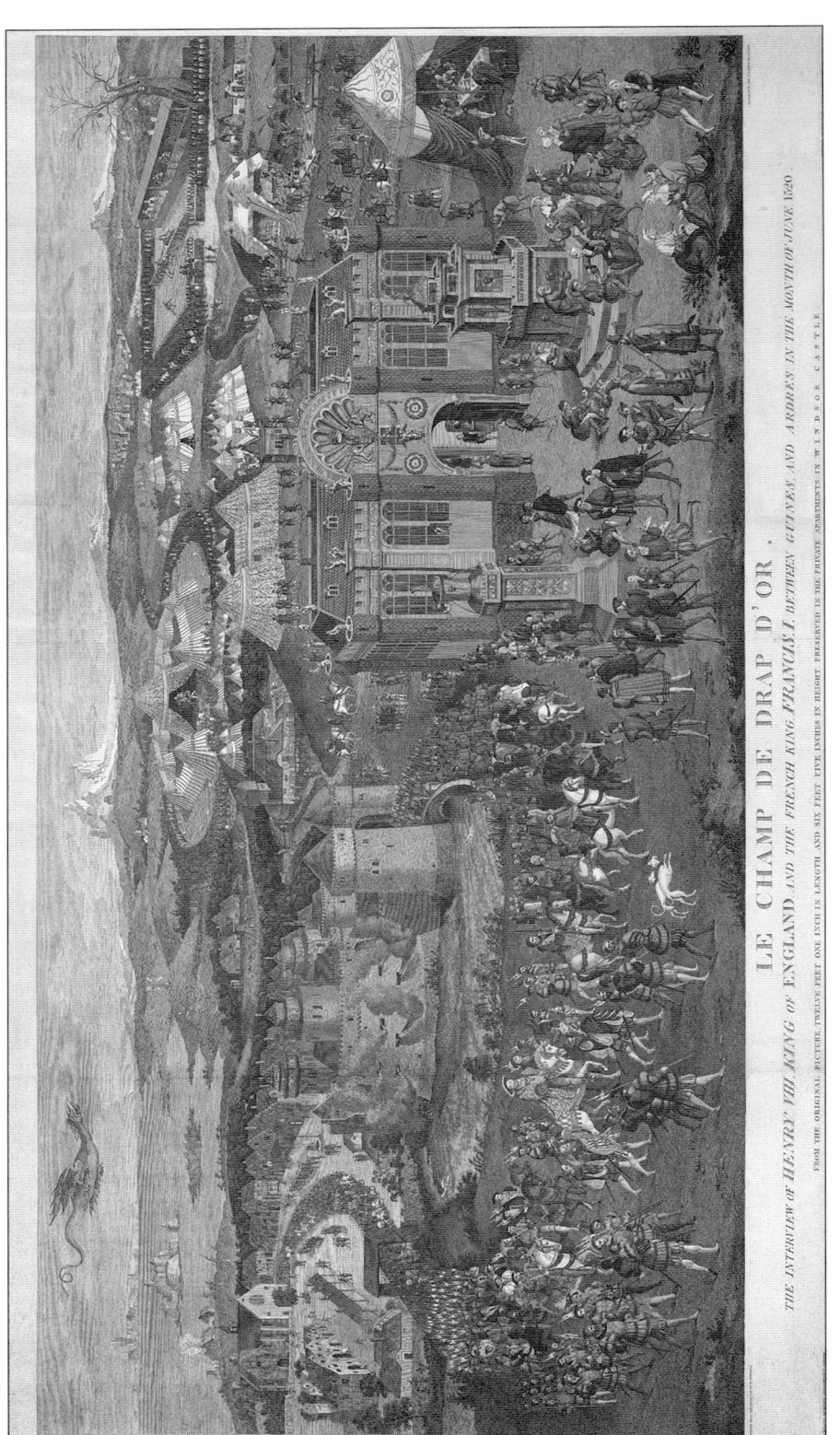

27. The Field of the Cloth of Gold. (*By Edward Edwards and James Basire after an Unknown Artist*)

was an ornate private chapel, a grand hall for entertaining, and even a cellar 'containing some 3,000 butts of the choicest wines in the world'. For added luxury, a series of windows was installed on the upper level all around the structure. They provided Henry and Katherine with splendid views of the wine-gushing fountains set up before the main gate, and of the Castle of Guînes in the distance. All in all, the palace was so stunning and well designed that it was said that even Leonardo da Vinci himself 'could not have done so well or so judiciously'.

When the French arrived at the valley, they too must have been impressed by Henry's palace. At the same time, they were equally curious about the much-talked-about King of England himself. Was he as majestic as was said? And was he as tall and handsome as King Francis? Anne Boleyn might have been able to tell them as she had probably once laid eyes on Henry VIII in person. Seven years ago, when he crossed the Channel to meet with the emperor to join forces with him against the French, Margaret of Austria, who went to Lille to meet up with her father, might well have brought Anne along. Whether or not she did, Claude and her ladies were able to see and judge for themselves on 7 June when Henry made his appearance that early evening. At a prearranged spot lined with spectators – both English and French – Henry and Francis rode forward from opposite sides and saluted each other. From what Claude and her countrymen could see, the English king lived up to his reputation. According to a description of him made just months ago by Sebastiano Giustiniani, Henry was

> much handsomer than any other sovereign in Christendom, a great deal handsomer than the King of France. He was very fair, and his whole frame admirably proportioned. Hearing that King Francis wore a beard, he allowed his own to grow, and as it was reddish, he had then got a beard which looked like gold.

After the two sovereigns embraced 'most lovingly', there was every expectation that the summit would be a success – and so it seemed. For the next eighteen days, there were rounds of celebrations and continuous declarations of friendship by Henry and Francis. They appeared to enjoy each other's company, but at the same time, being naturally competitive, they tried to outdo one another in athletic games and tournaments. But

Henry overplayed his hand when he challenged Francis to a wrestling match one day. Although he was bigger and physically stronger, his opponent, being lithe and slender, was able to escape Henry's clutches and pin *him* down instead to his great embarrassment. Not only did the two men – the sixteenth-century equivalent of today's 'alpha males' and 'frenemies' – try to outshine the other in sports, but also in courtesy. Even on the very first day of their meeting, the two kings made a great show of gallantry. After they had completed their salutations, they walked arm in arm towards a tent of cloth-of-gold to talk in private. At the vestibule, Francis insisted that Henry go in first. He refused, and said that it was the French king who must have the honour. Back and forth they went until Francis finally gave in and 'took precedence, without, however, once quitting the arm of King Henry'. On another occasion, Francis paid Henry an unexpected visit at the Castle of Guînes. After effusive greetings and doffing of hats, the French monarch announced that he had come to 'yield myself up to you as your prisoner, should you so wish it'. Returning the compliment, Henry led Francis into the dining hall for a feast.

The two queens were just as demonstrative. They exchanged gifts and fussed over giving priority to the other. But unlike their husbands, it was not to show off, but to be truly kind. During their time together presiding over and participating in entertainments or attending religious services, the pair got along very well. Still, perhaps Katherine despite herself, could not help but feel a tinge of jealousy when she was with her newly made friend. Claude had given Francis two sons already, and she was heavily pregnant yet again. Katherine on the other hand, only had a daughter Mary. Though Henry was still optimistic for boys, he and Katherine knew that with each passing year, the chances were becoming slimmer. If she did feel envious, Katherine said nothing, but genuinely hoped for the best for Claude, and no doubt for herself.

28. Katherine of Aragon. (*By G. P. Harding after an Unknown Artist*)

When two royal couples were not all together, they entertained separately. While Katherine of Aragon acted as hostess to Francis at Guînes, Henry visited the French ladies – Queen Claude, her sister-in-law Margaret of Angoulême, and her mother-in-law Louise of Savoy – at the Castle of Ardres. He and his men would often come with masks on, and the queen and her women were made to guess which one was Henry. He was fond of such antics. Back at home, he and his companions once disguised themselves as Robin Hood and his Merry Men to surprise his wife. An amused Katherine feigned astonishment and fright, and she allowed herself and her servants to be whisked away to a forest picnic. Claude too, knew how to react accordingly, and she gamely played along with Henry. Unless she confused his large frame with that of the Duke of Suffolk's, she was able to pick him out with ease, which would have pleased Henry's great vanity. As king, he would hardly blend in with mere commoners, even when disguised. After Claude's guests had all uncovered their faces, there was merriment and feasting. Might Henry have danced or conversed with Anne Boleyn on such evenings?

On the day before this 'eighth wonder of the world' was to conclude, an outdoor High Mass was officiated by Cardinal Wolsey in celebration of the new amity between France and England, and all present were given a plenary indulgence. When the service was done, a foundation stone was laid on the spot in anticipation of a

> beautiful church, entitled *Our Lady of Friendship* to be built, provided with sacerdotal ornaments, and endowed at the cost of the two kings; and such a number of chaplains is to be appointed as shall seem fit to them.

Upon its completion, it was Francis and Henry's intention to meet again there and often. When they finally parted the next day on 24 June, it was reported that both men were 'in tears … by reason of the tender love contracted by them reciprocally'.

Despite Francis's declaration shortly afterwards that he was 'on such loving terms with the King of England that he does not suppose there is any service in the world which the King of England would refuse him', the reality was that the two were no friendlier than before. Their meeting had been a great show for nothing. By the beginning of 1522, Francis was hearing rumours that Henry was double-crossing him through a secret alliance with his archenemy, the Hapsburgs. Indeed, a treaty between England and the Holy Roman Empire had been negotiated at Bruges by Cardinal Wolsey and none other than Margaret of Austria for a joint attack against France. As Francis became aware, England seemed to be preparing for war. English munitions were being shipped to Antwerp, and Henry's subjects living in Paris were told to come home. Among them, noted the French king, was 'the daughter of Mr Boullan'.

Chapter 4

It was duty that called Anne Boleyn abroad, and it was duty that called her home. Besides the increasing tensions between France and England, she was needed to settle a family dispute. Since the death of her great-grandfather, Thomas Butler, the Seventh Earl of Ormond, six years earlier, his heirs had been embroiled in a legal battle for his estate and title. Thomas Boleyn, as the son of Butler's daughter Margaret, laid claim to the legacy, but so did Sir Piers Butler. A relation of the late earl and a grandson of an Irish king no less, Butler also traced his ancestry to a previous holder of the Ormond title. The earldom was rightfully his, he argued, and taking advantage of laws of inheritance that favoured men over women, he pointed out that he was a male descendant of Thomas Butler, as opposed to Thomas Boleyn who would inherit through a female line.

29. Cardinal Thomas Wolsey. (*By Renold Elstrack*)

Normally the crown did not intrude in such matters, but as Piers Butler held considerable influence in Ireland, some settlement had to be reached between him and Thomas Boleyn. At the suggestion of the latter's brother-in-law, Thomas Howard, Earl of Surrey, the matter could be resolved by an alliance between the Butlers and the Boleyns. Sir Piers had a son named James who could marry Anne. Cardinal Wolsey, who already had the young man in his household, agreed, as did the king. Mistress Anne must return.

* * *

When Anne Boleyn stepped foot in England again in early 1522, it must have been a distant memory to her. Having spent a good part of her life overseas at the courts of Margaret of Austria and of Queen Claude, Anne returned more French than she was English. Having left at such a young age, she might well have spoken her native tongue with a trace of the second language she had learnt and excelled at. Certainly, she continued to write in French – an inscription in her *Book of Hours* spelt out '*le temps viendra, je Anne Boleyn*' ('the time will come, I Anne Boleyn') – and she read books in French as well. Later in life, Anne came into possession of a Bible *en Francoys*, and it was most dear to her as her chaplain William Latymer testified. She 'was very expert in the French tongue,' he said, 'exercising herself continually in reading the French Bible and other French books of like effect and conceived great pleasure in the same.' A visitor to the English court also noticed Anne's love for such devotional works:

> I am not surprised that you are never found, if circumstances permit, without your having some book in French in your hand which is of use and value in pointing out and finding the true and narrow way to all virtues ... I have seen you continually reading those helpful letters of Saint Paul which contain all the fashion and rule to live righteously, in every good manner of behaviour, which you know well and practise, thanks to your continual reading of them.

Every bit a French woman by upbringing, if not by birth, Anne was like a duck to water at Henry VIII's court. It was all the rage to be French. Not only were clothes and fine foods imported from France seen as more sophisticated and desirable, but so were the customs. A Venetian who visited England in 1514 remarked how 'the whole court now speaks both French and English'. There were even attempts to mimic the very conduct of Francis I's courtiers. Unlike the English who were sticklers for rules and decorum, their counterparts across the Channel were much more informal in the presence of their king. The sort of chumminess that Francis permitted his friends rubbed off on those in Henry's inner circle. These young gentlemen became 'so familiar and homely with him, and placed such light touches with him, that they forgot themselves'. But what was the norm at Fontainebleau was unacceptable at Greenwich. While the king did not have the heart to reprimand them himself, Cardinal Wolsey saw to it that these 'minions' were banished from the royal presence.

But Anne's French charms were never practised on her husband-to-be. Both the Boleyns and the Butlers eventually lost interest in the marriage alliance between them. Anne's father was allowed to claim the earldom of Ormond, while Piers Butler was given that of Ossory in compensation. As for James, he went on to wed a daughter of an Irish nobleman instead. Anne's own feelings towards the match and for James himself were never expressed, but it could be supposed that she was unenthusiastic to begin with. Although he seemed handsome enough as depicted by the artist Hans Holbein the Younger, this may not have been sufficient to win Anne's heart. After spending her formative years in the Netherlands and in France, she had been used to the high culture and lavish surroundings of the Hapsburgs and the Valois. Spoiled as such, the prospect of a new existence in Ireland far away from the glamour of courtly life was not something Anne would have looked forward to or have wanted for herself. There might also have been a yearning on Anne's part to chart her own path. She herself

30. James Butler. (*By Hans Holbein*)

had probably seen how Isabeau of Austria was made to marry a man she had never met and might never come to love, and what a dismal future there was in that. Despite the odds, Anne still hoped to steer the course of her own life. After all, Mary Tudor had defied convention to marry the man she loved. Might Anne too have envisioned such a possibility for herself?

* * *

When Anne arrived at the English court, it was said that she immediately turned heads. One of her first admirers was the courtier and poet, Sir Thomas Wyatt. According to his grandson George who later wrote about their relationship, Sir Thomas was instantly struck by 'the sudden appearance of this new beauty', and was enraptured by her 'witty and graceful speech'. While Anne was undoubtedly clever and eloquent thanks to her education and training abroad, Wyatt might have been overly generous as to Anne's looks. Beauty is in the eye of the beholder, and opinions among her contemporaries were mixed. During her lifetime, Anne received praise for being 'young and good looking', 'very beautiful', and 'beautiful and with an elegant figure', but it was not universal. A Venetian diplomat who saw Anne in person later on was unimpressed. 'Madam Anne is not one of the handsomest women in the world,' he sniffed. 'She is of middling stature, swarthy complexion, long neck, wide mouth, [and] bosom not much raised.' Despite his unenthusiasm, he did admit that her eyes – 'black and beautiful' – were seductive. Anne herself was well aware of their effect and she made good use of them,

> sometimes keeping them in repose, on other occasions, sending them forth as messengers, to carry the secret witness of the heart. Such was their power that many men were hers to command.

Even some of Anne's detractors, such as the Catholic clergyman and polemicist, Nicholas Sander (or Saunders), writing in the late sixteenth century, thought her 'handsome to look at, with a pretty mouth'. But Sander also claimed that Anne had an ugly 'large wen under her chin' which she took pains to hide, and 'on her right hand, six fingers'. The disfiguring swelling was probably derived from an unreliable hostile

31. Anne Boleyn. (*By an Unknown Artist*)

description of Anne, but there may have been some truth to an abnormality on her hand. In his biography of her, George Wyatt, who had 'gathered many notes touching this lady not without an intent to have opposed Saunders', did not wholly contradict him. According to his sources – his mother Jane Haute and one of Anne's long-time servants – she did indeed have a slight deformity. Nonetheless, it was trivial, just a small extra nail upon one of her fingers. Wyatt even waxed poetic about it saying that it was 'an occasion of greater grace to her hand, which with the tip of one of her other fingers, might be and was usually by her hidden without any blemish to it'.

Even if she was not a great beauty like the much-admired Mary Tudor, Anne stood out at the English court through her personality. She was sharp, accomplished, and high spirited. Again, Sander, who disliked Anne terribly and blamed her for much of the English Reformation, had to admit that she was the perfect courtier:

> she was amusing in her way, playing well on the lute, and was a good dancer. She was the model and mirror of those at court, for she was always well dressed, and every day made some change in the fashion of her garments.

Anne's allure therefore was not attributed solely to her looks, but also to her individuality and sense of style. She was also passionate and driven. But her single-mindedness and intensity would sometimes bring out her less attractive traits. In the hotbed of the Tudor court, Anne could be as ruthless as any of her adversaries. When she began to rise in prominence and power, she knew perfectly what the stakes were, and she was not afraid to play at the game of politics. So, while Anne could be kind-hearted and generous, she could also be ruthless and self-serving. Those who crossed her felt the brunt of her anger, and later in life, even Anne herself would admit that she lacked humility and was overbearing at times.

In tribute to Anne, Thomas Wyatt was said to have written verses to her and about her. One such poem (entitled *Anna*, or called that later on) went:

> *What word is that, that changeth not,*
> *Though it be turned and made in twain?*
> *It is mine answer, God it wot,*
> *And eke the only causer of my pain.*
> *A love that rewardeth with disdain,*
> *Yet is it loved. What would you more?*
> *It is my health eke, and my sore.*

If Anne was indeed the subject, she was disdainful of Wyatt, or at least she pretended to be by the conventions of courtly love. Popularized by Eleanor of Aquitaine (the wife of Louis VII of France and then of Henry II of England) in the twelfth century, this was a role-playing of idealized passion where a knight longed after a lady – usually of higher status than he – who was ultimately unattainable. Try as he might to woo her, she was forever scornful of him, but persist he must. Sometimes to complicate matters, the woman would already be spoken for, and thus the knight was even more lovelorn.

32. Sir Thomas Wyatt. (*By Francesco Bartolozzi after Hans Holbein*)

But in the case of Anne Boleyn and Thomas Wyatt, it was the latter who was already married. But he and Elizabeth Brooke were a miserable couple, and Thomas went on to cause a scandal by publicly accusing her of unfaithfulness and then living apart from her. When Thomas then found himself drawn to Anne, 'she rejected all his speech of love' on account of him having a wife. Nonetheless, Wyatt continued to pursue Anne, that is until he finally met his match in the form of an unexpected new rival.

Part II

Green grows the holly, so does the ivy
Though winter's blasts blow never so high.
As the holly grows green and never changes hue
So am I ever have been, unto my lady true.

From a song composed by Henry VIII

Chapter 5

In March 1522, England paid host to a delegation from the Holy Roman Empire. The envoys were not coming on behalf of Maximilian I, but his grandson. The old emperor had died in 1519, and Charles of Ghent was elected in his place. At just 18, Charles V, as he was now called, became the most powerful ruler in Europe. His dominions included Spain, the Netherlands, Germany, Austria, parts of Italy, and new lands across the Atlantic. Thanks to the close-knit world of monarchy, Charles was able to call himself a nephew of the King of England. Henry VIII's wife, Katherine of Aragon, was a sister of Charles's mother, Joanna of Castile. Shortly after his election, the new emperor had met with his uncle and aunt in England before they set sail for *The Field of the Cloth-of-Gold*. Charles, who had no love for Francis I, wanted to ensure that Henry was still friendly to the Hapsburgs. The Anglo-French alliance had cooled since the great conference, and now his English uncle was willing to forsake his treaty with Francis and even declare war with Charles upon their common foe.

To celebrate this new accord, festivities were held to welcome the Imperial ambassadors. On 2 March, there were jousts in which unrequited love was the theme. The king wore a suit of armour with a skirt embroidered *She hath wounded my heart*, while his companions adopted similar romantic mottos such as *No remedy* and *In prison I am in liberty and at liberty I am in prison*. In the past, such sentiments on Henry VIII's part were unequivocally

33. Medal of Charles V.
(*By Hans Reinhart the Elder*)

directed at Queen Katherine, as when he fought in her honour as *Sir Loyal Heart* at the birth of their short-lived son in 1511. But the king's love had diminished since then. Katherine had still not provided him with a male heir, and at 36, time was passing her by. As well, her looks were fading. She was becoming matronly in appearance, and she seemed even more so next to her husband, five years her junior. A diplomat who saw Katherine in person some years later described her being as 'not of tall stature, rather small. If not handsome she is not ugly; she is somewhat stout, and has always a smile on her countenance'. While Henry continued to acknowledge Katherine as his wife and queen, he did stray from her bed. Two of his mistresses were the Duke of Buckingham's sister and one Elizabeth – or rather 'Bessie' – Blount.

On 4 March, Cardinal Wolsey entertained the Imperial ambassadors at his palace of York Place. Situated along the Thames between the administrative centre of Westminster and the fashionable district of the well-to-do along the Strand, York Place was a monument in brick and mortar to the cardinal's power and prestige. The son of an Ipswich butcher, Wolsey had risen high through royal service beginning in the reign of Henry VII. His political acumen and his tireless efforts on behalf of the crown won the admiration of Henry VIII, who allowed Wolsey to run the tedious business of government in his place. While the king played, the cardinal worked, and it was a relationship that suited both of them fine. Thanks to his immense wealth accumulated through his various offices, Wolsey was able to expand York Place to his liking, and he was even rich enough to build himself a new episcopal palace named Hampton Court in Surrey. It was so grand and sumptuous that it surpassed anything that the king himself owned.

Worldly and congenial, Wolsey was a perfect host. He feted the envoys with a great banquet and arranged a masque for their pleasure. After they had dined, the cardinal's guests were brought to a chamber hung with tapestries and illuminated by torches. At the far end was the *Château Vert*, a large castle with three turrets. It was made of timber and covered over with paper painted to look like stone and with green tinfoil, giving the entertainment its name. Inside the structure were eight ladies, including Mary and Anne Boleyn dressed up as the personifications of *Kindness* and *Perseverance* respectively, and the king's sister as *Beauty*. The other five were attired as *Constancy*, *Bounty*, *Mercy*, *Pity*, and *Honour*. As the masque

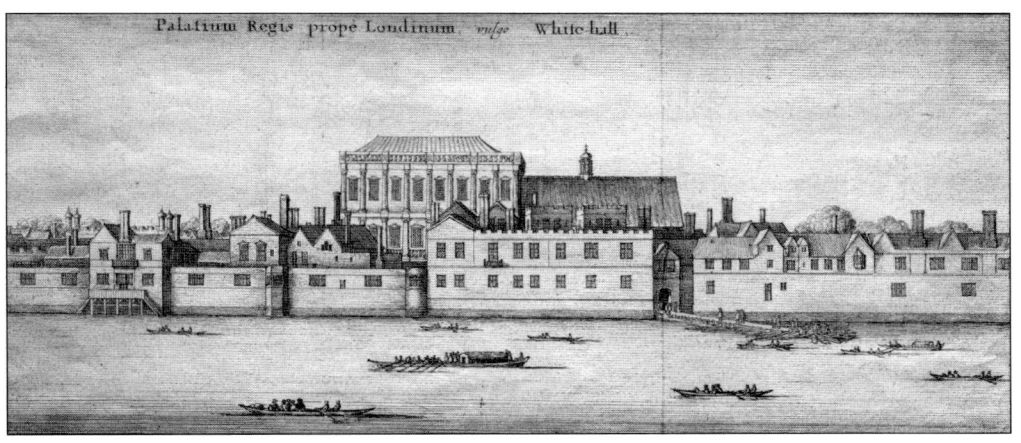

34. Whitehall Palace, Formerly York Place. (*By Wenceslaus Hollar*)

commenced, they were held captive by a band of 'women' from the Indies (actually 'children of my lord's chapel', that is Wolsey's choirboys in drag) disguised as *Danger, Disdain, Jealousy, Unkindness, Scorn, Strangeness*, and *Malebouche* (*Evil Tongue*). Then suddenly, *Ardent Desire*, in a shimmering outfit of 'crimson satin with burning flames of gold', brought in *Amorous* (King Henry) and his companions *Nobleness, Youth, Attendance, Loyalty, Pleasure, Gentleness*, and *Liberty*. They demanded that the gaolers give up the castle and free the ladies. When they refused, *Amorous* and his troupe laid siege to the *Château Vert* as a 'great peal of guns' was shot outside the palace. The Indian ladies threw 'comfits' (confections) and rose water to defend themselves, while their assailants bombarded them with oranges, dates, and other fruits. After what was essentially a food fight, the choirboys surrendered, allowing *Amorous* and his band to free the prisoners. Each chose a partner and they danced together. Afterwards, all the participants removed their disguises, and the celebrations continued on into the night.

* * *

Sometime after her return to England, Anne Boleyn received a post in the queen's household. The coveted position was obtained through the help of her father Sir Thomas. As a valued courtier and envoy, Boleyn used his influence to make 'such means that she was admitted to be one of Queen Katherine's maids'. Anne's mother might have spoken on her behalf too. Lady Boleyn had formerly been in royal service and was well regarded. Years ago, when Katherine was unable to attend the christening of her niece, Frances Brandon, the daughter of the Duke and Duchess of Suffolk, she had Elizabeth stand in for her. After Anne was placed, Katherine probably came to like the young woman. She had been well trained in France as a maid-of-honour to Queen Claude, and on a more personal note, Anne too had an affection for Katherine's former sister-in-law, Margaret of Austria.

Katherine of Aragon's court was not dissimilar to that of Claude's. Both queens were known for their goodness and piety, and as such, Katherine fostered an environment where high morals were paramount. Her servants, including Mistress Anne, were expected to be of upstanding character and fine deportment. They were to be obedient, loyal, and modest, and always suitably dressed, especially when they appeared with their mistress in public. As she had done for Queen Claude, Anne waited upon Katherine, looking to her wants and needs. Because she had newly arrived in the queen's service, she was most likely not placed within the more intimate space of the royal bedchamber, which was reserved for Katherine's most favourite servants who had been with her for years already. Instead, Anne would have been one of the thirty or so ladies joining their mistress as she presided over court, received visitors, attended worship, and other such functions. When Anne and her companions were not called for, they were put under the watchful eye of one of the more senior ladies who saw to it that they were always on their best behaviour even when they were not in the presence of the queen. Frivolity and idle talk were frowned upon, and the maids were encouraged to spend their time productively in recreations such as practicing needlework, playing music, or reading books of an educational or inspirational nature.

Of course, the presence of gentlemen in the queen's chambers was discouraged. Unless they had some specific duty there, they had no reason being about, especially around the ladies. But warnings and reprimands did little to put off the young bucks such as Henry Percy, the son of the Earl of Northumberland. Whenever Cardinal Wolsey came to court on the king's business, Percy, who was brought up in his house like James Butler was, would 'resort for his pastime unto the queen's chamber, and there fall in dalliance among the queen's maidens'. He came to notice

Anne, and his feelings for her were soon reciprocated. Far from being a flirtation or a sexual tryst, the relationship blossomed into a true romance, so much that the lovers might even have formally pledged themselves to one another with the intent to marry.

But word got out to the cardinal. Wolsey was still resolved on matching Anne to James Butler, and when he heard how she and Percy were thwarting his plans, he was incensed. He summoned the young man for a dressing down, and to make it even more humiliating for Percy, Wolsey berated him in public. He scolded Percy for his 'peevish folly' in entangling himself with 'a foolish girl yonder in the court' without his permission and that of the king's. As he was heir 'to one of the most worthiest earldoms of this realm', Wolsey continued, his marriage was an affair of state to be decided upon by his elders. And besides that, Anne had already been claimed by another. The cardinal's anger reduced the 'wilful boy', as he called Percy, to tears. In his defence, the young man exclaimed that he considered himself to be of proper age and means to support a wife. And as to Wolsey's dismissal of Anne as a nobody, Percy reminded him that although 'she be a simple maid, and having but a knight to her father', she was also descended from the Duke of Norfolk and the Earl of Ormond, thus making her pedigree as good as his own. But seeing that the cardinal and the king would have it so, Percy renounced Anne and promised to have nothing to do with her anymore. Broken by Wolsey and by his father, the Earl of Northumberland, who came down from the north to upbraid him on his responsibilities, Percy went on to marry the daughter of the Earl of Shrewsbury as he was told to do.

But Anne was made of sterner stuff. She shed no tears as Percy did, but instead was said to be 'greatly offended'. Those who heard her rants against Wolsey would hardly have taken her seriously. Anne had been foolish as he said, and as punishment, she was banished from court and sent back to Hever for a spell. But far from being contrite, Anne 'smoked' and continued in her hatred of Wolsey, vowing 'that if it lay ever in her power, she would work the cardinal as much displeasure' as he did to her.

* * *

The beautiful gardens of Hever Castle were a perfect setting for a great romance. As told by the Italian author Gregorio Leti, it was there that

Henry VIII first met Anne Boleyn. He was struck by her loveliness and charm, and they talked for an hour together. Later when he returned to his palace, Henry could not contain his excitement and he told Wolsey all about his encounter with this remarkable young lady who possessed 'the soul of an angel and was worthy of a crown'.

It was a sweet story, not unlike the king's first sighting of Anne at a ball given by the cardinal as told in William Shakespeare's play *Henry VIII*, but as Leti was writing in the seventeenth century, his account may have been apocryphal. What is known is that Anne had seen the king before

35. King Henry the Eighth and Anna Bullen. (*By William Hogarth*)

– probably in Lille in 1513 and certainly at *The Field of the Cloth-of-Gold* in 1520 – though whether Henry himself had even noticed her then is a mystery. But by the time Anne had established herself at his court and was acting as one of his wife's ladies-in-waiting, Henry did become aware of her and he was soon besotted. George Cavendish, Wolsey's gentleman usher, who was the source of Anne's affair with Henry Percy, was certain that their relationship was broken up by Wolsey by direct order of the king. It was not because Henry was concerned about preserving the Boleyn–Butler alliance, but because he wanted Anne for himself. If this was true, his wooing of her began sometime after her punitive exile at Hever.

With Henry Percy out of the picture, the king still had to contend with Thomas Wyatt. After her return to court, Anne allowed herself to be pursued by the poet again, despite her earlier disdain for him. Perhaps Wyatt's continuing estrangement from his wife made Anne more receptive to his advances, or she was simply playacting at courtly love again. On one occasion, Anne, taking a cue from Margaret of Austria, allowed Wyatt to steal a jewelled tablet from her, which he then wore concealed around his neck as a love token. Subsequently, she let the king, who was also vying for her favour, snatch a ring off of her. One day at a game of bowls, it was undecided which toss – Wyatt's or Henry's – had won. The king, declaring himself the victor, exclaimed, 'I tell thee, it is mine,' as he gestured to Anne's ring now set upon his finger. Undeterred, Wyatt took out her jewel and using the lace from which it was suspended, measured the distance of the bowls and was made the winner instead. Henry recognized the tablet as Wyatt knew he would, and he went away in a huff, grumbling that he had been tricked and 'so broke up the game'.

The king's irritation was a warning to Wyatt to stay clear of Anne. Knowing he could not compete – or dare to – against such a rival, he withdrew. Wyatt lamented his loss in verse, comparing Anne to a wild creature of which only Caesar (that is King Henry) could catch:

> *Who list her hunt, I put him out of doubt,*
> *As well as I may spend his time in vain:*
> *And, graven with diamonds in letters plain*
> *There is written, her fair neck round about:*
> *Noli me tangere, for Caesar's I am,*
> *And wild for to hold, though I seem tame.*

Determined to make Anne his – and his alone – Henry began romancing her with love letters. They were undated, but it is believed that he started sending them around the autumn of 1526. The king hated writing – it was 'somewhat tedious and painful' as he once complained to Wolsey, but to convey his most intimate thoughts and feelings to Anne, and to keep his correspondence private, he put pen to paper himself. Henry wrote in both English and French to 'the woman in the world that I value the most', declaring himself as Anne's 'loyal servant'. Apart from being expressions of love, the letters allowed Henry to communicate with her from a distance. Perhaps on the advice of her family to play hard to get, Anne had withdrawn herself from court leaving Henry to beg her not to 'let absence lessen your affection to us … for it were a great pity to increase their pain, which absence alone does sufficiently'. But seeing that 'I cannot be present in person with you', his gift of a bracelet with his picture inside had to suffice. Anne was clearly acting aloof, as in another letter the king mentioned how he had not heard back from her in a very long time, and that she 'would neither come to court with my lady, your mother, nor any other way'.

Anne's sudden departure to Hever had put the king in perplexity. Before she left, she had given him the impression that she welcomed his advances, but when she was gone, Henry wondered why she had 'entirely changed the opinion in which I left you?' Was Anne simply going by the playbook of courtly love by blowing hot and cold, or was she 'embarrassed at first at having hooked this great fish', as one of her modern biographers opined, and was unsure on how to handle such a suitor?

At age 35 – years before his descent into obesity and cruelty – Henry Tudor was a magnificent specimen of a man. He was handsome, athletic, and intelligent. When he came to the throne, a new age had dawned in England, gushed one of his courtiers: 'our king does not set his heart on gold or jewels, but on virtue, glory, and immortality!' Anne too, no doubt, was not immune to his charms. Apart from his good looks, she was drawn to his inner qualities as well. Henry had received an excellent education in his youth and his knowledge was diverse. He was interested in theology, astronomy, warfare, politics, literature, and art and architecture. He was even a skilled musician, with a talent for singing, playing, and composing.

While Anne may have found herself attracted to Henry VIII, she may have at the same time, taken offence to being his mistress. She knew

36. A Courtly Couple. (*By Hans Holbein*)

how such women were easily used and discarded, and she had no interest in being one of his flings. In 1519, after Bessie Blount had given birth to his illegitimate son, Henry Fitzroy, the king ended their relationship by marrying her off to another. Henry then moved on to Anne's sister. Mary Boleyn had been wed to the courtier William Carey since 1520, but that did not prevent her – apparently with her husband's consent – from having sex with the king as well. Mary would later have two children, Katherine and Henry, and because of her extramarital affair, there has been speculation that one or both of them might have been Henry VIII's. Whoever the father was, shortly after young Henry Carey's birth in March 1526, the king was no longer seeing Mary, but was in hot pursuit of her sister instead.

Anne may also have had no desire to be the 'other woman'. She may have respected the queen – and herself – too much to be put in the middle of Katherine of Aragon's relationship with her husband. When they appeared in public together, the king and queen still seemed to be the happy and devoted couple as they were when they wed in 1509. But the reality was that the marriage was fraying. While Henry continued to honour Katherine as queen, it was an open secret that they had ceased having sexual relations. The king no longer found his ageing wife appealing, and it was evident that after a series of stillborn or short-lived children (except for the Princess Mary), Katherine could no longer bear him another child. Her last pregnancy was years ago, in 1518, and sadly, it was a girl born dead.

By the 1520s, Henry was desperate for a son. Recalling his lessons, he had been taught in his youth about the history of England, he knew how disastrous it would be if he left no male heir to continue the Tudor dynasty. In the twelfth century, when his ancestor King Henry I died and left the kingdom to his daughter Maude (Matilda), the country was engulfed by civil war. As a female, her rule was never accepted, and her cousin Stephen of Blois was made king instead. But a disputed succession was not a peril relegated to the distant past. Seventy years ago, England was again swallowed up in war when the rival Houses of Lancaster and York both asserted their right to the crown. The conflict would last over thirty years and claim the lives of three kings – Henry VI, Richard III, and probably Edward V – before Henry VII, a Lancastrian, finally put an end to it at Bosworth Field. He united the warring factions by marrying the Yorkist princess, Elizabeth of York, and establishing the new dynasty of the Tudors.

37. Henry Fitzroy, Duke of Richmond.
(*By Harding and Clamp after Lucas Horenbout*)

While there was actually no law in England to prevent a woman from assuming queenship in her own right, such an innovation had never been put into practice. Maude, as mentioned, had been rejected, and more recently, when Henry VII took the throne, the arguably stronger claims of his own mother Margaret Beaufort and of his wife Elizabeth were never considered. Henry VIII himself was of the same thinking that women as the weaker sex should not rule. Even though his daughter Princess Mary had received an excellent education and was even sent to Ludlow in the Welsh Marches for a time to hold court as his nominal successor, Henry could not see his way in making Mary a future queen.

He was so obsessed with leaving a son on his throne that it was said that the king considered tampering with the laws of inheritance. In 1525, he took the extraordinary step of making his bastard son, Henry Fitzroy, Duke of Richmond and Somerset. Such great titles implied that the boy was meant for bigger things ahead, and there were rumours that his father intended to make Fitzroy king one day despite his illegitimacy. However, this plan, even if it was given serious thought, was ultimately abandoned. Whatever his intentions were, Katherine of Aragon, who was naturally protective of her daughter, was highly resentful of Fitzroy's elevation. A furious argument ensued between the royal couple, but in the end, Katherine 'was obliged to submit and to have patience'.

Chapter 6

Because his wife could give him no living sons, Henry VIII turned to Scripture for answers. In *The Book of Leviticus*, he stumbled upon passages that forbade a man to 'uncover the nakedness' of his brother's wife and to take her in marriage as it was an 'unclean thing'. By such a transgression, they would be childless. Henry of course had a daughter, but being a girl, Mary did not count; nor did a directive from *Deuteronomy* which actually encouraged marrying one's widowed sister-in-law as to continue the family line. And there was also the question of Katherine's virginity. Even though the Vatican had given her and Henry a dispensation to wed, this was upon the assumption that her union with Arthur Tudor had not been consummated. The couple had lived as man and wife for almost six months until the prince's death, but as Katherine swore, they had never known each other in the fullest sense of the word. Despite her insistence that she came to Henry's bed *virgo intacta*, he was still convinced that God had cursed their union. As he must have a son, Henry made the fateful decision to end his marriage and to take a new wife.

But was it truly the king himself who had come to this resolution? Critics of his *Great Matter*, as the divorce – or the annulment – came to be called, had also pointed their fingers at Cardinal Wolsey and at Anne Boleyn. Queen Katherine herself was of the opinion that it was the wily churchman who was the author of her woes on account of his personal malice towards her. Wolsey would fiercely deny this in a confrontation with the queen, 'but whatsoever was said, she believed him not'. Katherine's refusal to blame her own husband was understandable as it was easier for her to think that he was being manipulated by the cardinal, than that he was mistreating her of his own accord.

If not Wolsey, Anne was said to be the instigator of Katherine's troubles. Reginald Pole, a cousin of Henry VIII and later Archbishop of Canterbury, was adamant that it was Mistress Boleyn who put the thought in his head, as he would later tell the king in no uncertain terms:

38. Reginald Pole, Later Archbishop of Canterbury. (*By Pieter van Gunst after Adriaen van der Werff*)

She, indeed, has said that she will make herself available to you on one condition alone. You must reject your wife whose place she desires to hold. This modest woman does not want to be your concubine! She wants to be your wife. I believe that she learned from the example of her sister, if in no other way, how quickly you can have your fill of concubines.

However, Pole was then writing from Italy, and his information came from second-hand sources eager to paint Anne as a villainess in the king's *Great Matter*. Not only was she a virago, she was also a lady of loose morals as her sister Mary was perceived to be. But in reality, it is difficult to believe that Anne was in such a position that she was able to force Henry to turn his kingdom topsy-turvy for her sake. The decision must ultimately have been his. But if Anne was not the mastermind of the king's divorce proceedings, she was undoubtedly a key player as events unfolded.

Anne may have been told of Henry's intentions and what that meant for her at the end of 1526. In place of what she had probably considered to be an unappealing offer to make her his mistress, Henry was now promising to crown her queen. If Anne was somewhat in love with Henry already, the prospect of being his wife would be gratifying. Anne has often been faulted for her ambition, but that was largely in response to her sex. As a female, her contemporaries thought her overly proud, and even centuries later, writers such as Agnes Strickland blamed her for being a woman 'in whom vanity and ambition were the leading traits'. As a strait-laced Victorian, Strickland even compared Anne to Poppea, the conniving wife of the Roman emperor Nero: 'that her love was not an affair of the heart, but a matter of diplomacy.' But such criticism was unfair, and was in keeping with the meek and mild conduct expected of her sex.

Anne's drive was an attestation of her upbringing. Thomas Boleyn had been a self-made man and he expected his children to be successful too. In that resolve, he

39. Medal of Henry VIII in 1526. (*By Hans Daucher*)

had sent Anne and Mary out into the world, and he had found George a place at court to make good as well. Sir Thomas could never have imagined such a great future for Anne, and when he was told by the king what his intentions for his daughter were, he was reported as being 'not a little joyful' at the news. As for the lady herself, the thought of being Queen of England must have been dazzling. Apart for its worldly advantages and rewards, Anne, as a religious individual, viewed her good fortune as part of a divine plan for herself as she would later state. Convinced that she was called to be queen, Anne accepted the king's proposal. She would be his – 'body and heart' – as he wanted.

Anne's surrender was conveyed to Henry VIII by means of a gift. On New Year's Day 1527, she sent the king a jewel – a 'handsome diamond and ship in which the lonely damsel is tossed about'. Anne had apparently sent no written message with it, but to Henry, her meaning was clear: she was looking to him as her safe harbour. Not only did he thank her for the present itself, but 'chiefly for the fine interpretation and too humble submission which your goodness had made in this case'. At the bottom of his letter, Henry scribbled 'H seeks AB no other,' and around Anne's initials, he drew a lover's heart.

Soon, Henry and Anne's relationship became more physically intimate, and he was writing about being in 'my sweetheart's arms, whose pretty ducks I trust shortly to kiss'. But embraces and the fondling of Anne's breasts seemed to be as far as Henry was willing to go for the time being. As he wanted a legitimately born son, he had no choice but to hold off on full intercourse until he and Anne were properly married. The happy day, they both assumed, would be in the very near future. In the meanwhile, they kept the queen in the dark as Anne resumed her place among her ladies.

On 5 May, Katherine of Aragon entertained ambassadors from France in her chambers. Her husband and Francis I were friends again and they wanted to match their children – Princess Mary and the Duke of Orléans – together to seal the recently concluded Treaty of Westminster. As

40. Self Portrait (by Hans Holbein).

Mary danced with one of the French representatives, Henry chose Anne Boleyn as his partner. At the continuation of the revels the next day, Anne, who had performed in the pageant of the *Château Vert*, may have been a participant in a new masque staged for the French guests. The king was eager to impress them, and a new banqueting house had been constructed at the Palace of Greenwich. Inside was a great hall shaped like an amphitheatre. The floor was covered with silken cloth embroidered with lilies in tribute to the French, and the ceiling – designed by the king's astronomer Nicholas Kratzer in conjunction with Hans Holbein – was decorated with an immense painting of a map of the world and the signs of the zodiac. After the audience was seated, an allegory of the *Dispute of Love and Riches* was presented. The gods Cupid and Plutus made their arguments as to who was the mightier, and a mock battle was fought. Eight young ladies (perhaps Anne one of them) dressed in cloth-of-gold and wearing jewelled garlands danced before the assembly. A Venetian who was present thought them to be 'of such rare beauty as to be supposed goddesses rather than human beings'.

The reception of the French had been a splendid affair and Queen Katherine played the warm and welcoming hostess, albeit with a heavy heart. She had always envisioned the Tudors allied to the Hapsburgs with her daughter Mary wed to the emperor, but events of late had conspired against her. In spite of their family ties, Charles V had jilted Mary for a Portuguese princess instead. The international situation had also changed with England joined to France once again. Katherine might also have been troubled by rumours about her husband and Mistress Anne. Although they made efforts to keep their relationship quiet, the queen might have heard that he had taken her up as his new lover.

By 18 May, Katherine's worries were confirmed and it was worse than she believed: Cardinal Wolsey had set up a secret commission to consider the validity of her marriage. The king himself had been summoned to appear, and as a dutiful son of the Church, he consented to the inquiry. But word got out, and as Don Inigo de Mendoza, the Imperial ambassador, reported, Katherine was 'so full of apprehension on this account' that she dared not even speak to him about it. She had to communicate her fears through an intermediary who had to pretend he did not come from the queen herself. Katherine was convinced that it was a plot of Wolsey's making, never suspecting that her husband of eighteen years had anything

41. The Ball. (*By Cornelis Anthonisz*)

to do with it. But Mendoza learnt the truth that it was Henry who was 'so bent on this divorce'; Wolsey was merely his hatchet man.

For the next month, Katherine carried on as if nothing was amiss as 'no intimation or summons had up to that date been made to the queen' by the king or the cardinal. But finally, on 22 June, Henry decided that he must tell her the truth. Screwing up his courage for what he knew would be a difficult and unpleasant confrontation, he announced to Katherine that they could no longer be man and wife:

they had been in mortal sin during all the years they had lived together, and that this being the opinion of many canonists and theologians whom he had consulted on the subject, he had come to the resolution, as his conscience was much troubled thereby, to separate himself from her.

Nevertheless, she would be well taken care of as 'Princess Dowager' and as his sister-in-law, and Henry asked Katherine where she would like to retire to?

The queen was stunned. She had no answer to all that he said, much less where she was to go. She burst into tears. Equally agitated, Henry made an awkward attempt to console her. 'All should be done for the best,' he said, and for the present, she must not mention any of this to anyone. Katherine, he knew, was extremely popular with the people, and there were bound to be demonstrations on her behalf. Furthermore, she had her powerful nephew, the emperor, in her corner. He would certainly come to her aid for their family honour. And then there was also the papacy to consider. Katherine would surely appeal to the Vatican, which had given her the dispensation to marry her late husband's brother.

As expected, the queen sought Charles's help. Since she was carefully watched, Katherine resorted to deception. She arranged for a servant named Francisco Felipez, on the pretext of visiting his sick mother in Spain, to go to the emperor instead. Along the way, Felipez was able to evade capture – Henry had not been fooled – and make his way to Valladolid by the end of July. Charles V was as astonished as Katherine was, and he leapt to her defence. As he wrote to Mendoza, 'we cannot desert the queen, our good aunt, in her troubles, and intend doing all we can in her favour.' Meanwhile, the ambassador was instructed not to provoke the king and hope that he would come to his senses. But in case things were to go badly for the queen in 'this ugly affair', Charles would ask the pope to 'persuade the king and his ministers to put a stop to the evils which must necessarily arise out of so scandalous a business'. Additionally, he would request that the Vatican withdraw Cardinal Wolsey's legatine powers, preventing him from ruling on the annulment in England.

Charles was certain that His Holiness would be amenable. Not only would Pope Clement VII uphold Queen Katherine as a good woman who was properly married in the eyes of the Church, but also because he was effectively a prisoner of his. In 1526, the pope had formed an alliance with certain city states and with the French to halt Imperial expansion into Italy. But in May 1527, mercenaries in the pay of the emperor got out of hand. They sacked Rome and laid waste to the city. Some 8,000 people were slaughtered 'of all nationalities being indiscriminately put to the sword or subjected to the most atrocious torture', including clergymen. Those who were spared were taken prisoner and held for ransom. The pope himself was fired upon with artillery, and he only evaded capture by fleeing to the Castel Sant'Angelo. His palace had been entirely gutted and turned into stables by the invaders, and even the Church of Saint Peter itself was vandalized. It was plundered to the shock of Christendom, and 'many dead bodies lay about, so much disfigured that it was impossible to recognize them, and in the chapel itself, close to the altar of Saint Peter, were great pools of blood'.

42. Medal of Pope Clement VII. (*By an Unknown Artist*)

43. The Siege of Castel Sant'Angelo in Rome, 1527. (*By Dirck Volckertsz*)

Chapter 7

To build up his case, Henry VIII gave no indication that he was passionately in love with another woman, only that his conscience troubled him for marrying his brother's widow. The official line, 'as was devised' between the king and the cardinal at a meeting that summer at York Place, was that Henry had been made aware of the possible illegality of his marriage by the French. During the negotiations for Princess Mary's hand, the ambassador, the Bishop of Tarbes, had raised the question of her legitimacy due to the unusual circumstances of her parents' marriage. It was because of the bishop's concerns that Henry was determined 'to discover the truth'. He had no desire to cast away his beloved queen of so many years, but should it be found that Katherine was indeed not his wife by law, he would make a new match to secure the succession with King Francis's sister-in-law – and Anne Boleyn's old friend – Renée of France.

No mention was made of Anne who was being kept discreetly in the background, but Wolsey knew that once the king was free, he would make her his new wife – not Renée – as he was letting on. While a French marriage would have been acceptable to Wolsey who had never liked the Hapsburgs, he shuddered at the prospect of Anne as queen. He remembered how she had blamed him for breaking up her relationship with Henry Percy, and he might have heard how she had sworn vengeance against him. At the time, Wolsey would have dismissed Anne's grievances as those of an immature lovesick girl whose heart had been broken, but now she was the king's darling. No good would come from such a union. Putting aside the queen would provoke the emperor and risk a schism with Rome. Furthermore, Katherine was much loved by the people. There were still those who remembered her as a lovely young princess from Spain come to wed Arthur Tudor, and how after his untimely death, she had suffered much deprivation at the hands of the miserly Henry VII. And when she was finally Queen of England, there was never such a valiant woman. When the Scots invaded in 1513, it was Katherine as regent who rallied the English troops and urged them on to victory. She was also the lady merciful. When the London apprentices were condemned to death by Henry VIII for rioting on what came to be called Evil May Day in 1517, it was Katherine who begged him on her knees to spare them. Owing to her long popularity, any attempt to remove her would be an uphill battle, Wolsey sighed.

Faced with such difficulties, the cardinal tried to dissuade the king from his reckless course. He even knelt to him begging him to reconsider, but to no avail. In early July, when Wolsey set out to France to conclude the new peace, he was also ordered to smooth the way to the royal divorce by canvassing support from leading clerics. On his way to Dover, Wolsey met with William Warham, the Archbishop of Canterbury, and with John Fisher, the Bishop of Rochester, assuring them of the king's good and honest intentions in wanting a new marriage. They were not told about his lust for Anne Boleyn of course. And once in France, the cardinal was to continue his efforts towards the divorce. He was to secure the pope's release by brokering a truce with the emperor. Once Clement was free from Charles's clutches, he could pronounce in Henry VIII's favour. Failing that, Wolsey was to make an extraordinary request of the pontiff. He would ask Clement to grant him powers to hold a conclave at Avignon – effectively making him an *ersatz* pope – with the authority to pronounce on the King of England's marriage.

44. William Warham, Archbishop of Canterbury. (*By Francesco Bartolozzi after Hans Holbein*)

Even with Henry's grandiose schemes for Wolsey, he and Anne did not entirely trust the cardinal. They were aware of his misgivings and worried that he would not be fully committed to their cause. As a backup, the king sent one of his secretaries, William Knight, to confer with the pope on a 'secret affair, which is to me only committed' as Knight called it, without

Wolsey's knowledge. Once he was able to make his way to the besieged Clement, Knight was to ask His Holiness for a dispensation allowing his master to take an unnamed lady – Anne of course – as his new wife to whom he was considered related to in the eyes of the Church; Henry had once been sexually intimate with her sister Mary. Such a marriage could then take place even before the king was officially set free from Queen Katherine. In other words, Henry was requesting permission to commit bigamy. It was a bizarre request, but once Clement had given it his blessing, it was one step closer to making Anne queen.

45. Sir William Fitzwilliam. *(By Francesco Bartolozzi after Hans Holbein)*

Wolsey was entirely blindsided. Knight's letter to him announcing his impending journey to the Continent was a warning to the cardinal that he was losing the king's confidence. And when Knight showed up at his doorstep on his way to Italy, he did not let Wolsey in on his mission, giving the cardinal even more unease that much was being kept from him. What Wolsey did know was that circumstances were not boding well for himself. While in France, he had failed to appease the emperor for the pope's release, and he was equally unsuccessful in obtaining Clement's consent for him to hold at papal court at Avignon. Furthermore, as the courtier Sir William Fitzwilliam warned Wolsey, while he was away, the king had gathered about him those who were no friend to him. During the summer, Henry VIII had spent much time in the company of Lady Anne's father Thomas Boleyn (now Viscount Rochford), her uncle the Duke of Norfolk (formerly the Earl of Surrey), and other nobles who had also long resented the cardinal for his rise from rags to riches. Even the Duke of Suffolk, whom Wolsey had once helped to regain the king's favour after his marriage to his sister, now showed his true colours by turning against him.

Wolsey felt great trepidation when he returned to England in late September. He was given an inkling of what to expect when he arrived at Richmond Palace to a debriefing with the king. The cardinal, as was

46. Richmond Palace. (*By Wenceslaus Hollar*)

the custom, sent a messenger to ask Henry VIII where he would receive him. But it was not the king who answered, but his mistress. Speaking on his behalf, Anne said haughtily, 'Where else is the cardinal to come? Tell him that he may come here, where the king is!' If Henry was taken aback by her audacity, he did not show it but only muttered in agreement. Upon receiving the answer, Wolsey was reported as being 'extremely annoyed'. Whereas once he had unfettered access to the king, he now found Mistress Anne as his self-appointed gatekeeper. When Wolsey finally greeted Henry, he 'dissembled as much as he could, and concealed his resentment', as a gloating Anne looked on.

Later that year, Wolsey must have derived satisfaction on hearing that William Knight had been no more successful than he was in facilitating the king's divorce. Clement VII, weak willed and still afraid of the emperor, had given the King of England the dispensation he wanted so much, but not entirely. Upon a careful reading of the document, Henry was granted permission to marry the sister of his former mistress only upon the condition that he was free of Queen Katherine first. Henry was furious in being duped.

In February 1528, another attempt was made to sway the pope. Two emissaries, Stephen Gardiner and Edward Fox, were sent to the town of Orvieto where Clement VII had escaped to two months earlier. It was hoped that with the pope freed from the Imperialists, he would be more agreeable to Henry VIII's demands. When the two Englishmen reached Clement at his papal court-in-exile in March, they found him in a wretched state. Orvieto was remote with goods and supplies hard to come by, and it was prone to pestilence in the summer. Clement had taken refuge in the local bishop's run-down palace where 'hunger, scarcity, bad lodgings, and ill air' keep him much confined as he had been in the Castel Sant'Angelo. His conditions were so pitiful that Clement lamented that his 'captivity at Rome was better than liberty here'. After three weeks of negotiations with the pope – Gardiner and Fox feared to stay longer in case of plague – it was agreed that Clement would send a representative to try the divorce with Cardinal Wolsey. But beyond that, he could do no more, Clement said, for fear of offending the emperor.

47. Stephen Gardiner, Bishop of Winchester. (*By Sylvester Harding and W.N. Gardiner*)

* * *

Until the *Great Matter* was resolved, Henry, Katherine, and Anne lived together in an awkward *ménage à trois*. Anne returned to serving the queen who by this time was well aware that her lady-in-waiting had become her rival for the king's love. Instead of confronting Anne or ejecting her from her household altogether, Katherine affected an air of indifference. She even went out of her way, it was said, to hold 'Mistress Anne in more estimation for the king's sake', displaying no 'spark or kind of grudge or displeasure'. By not giving Anne the satisfaction that she was troubled at all, allowed Katherine to keep her dignity and to maintain the illusion that all was well between her and her husband. She would even invite Anne to play cards with her. But as George Wyatt explained, Katherine had an ulterior motive. It was a means to keep Anne occupied and away from Henry. One time when the two ladies sat down, Katherine hinted – or rather warned – Anne that she knew more than she let on. After her opponent had won a round by picking up a king card, Katherine gave her a knowing look and remarked, 'My Lady

Anne, you have good hap to stop at a king. But you are not like others; you will have all or nothing.'

With the queen declaring herself an adversary, Anne thought it wise to make Wolsey a friend. Even though the cardinal had been a disappointment so far in his handling of the divorce, he could still be a good asset, Anne thought, if they were working together rather than apart. Putting aside her grudge, she began making overtures to Wolsey. She wrote him loving letters, praising his wisdom and his efforts in helping her and the king. Soon, Anne was on such familiar terms with the cardinal that she was able to sweet-talk him into obtaining little favours. Would His Lordship be so kind, she once asked, to let her have some delicious carps and shrimps from his ponds, and for her mother, some tunny fish?

All was going well for Anne. She now had an ally in the cardinal, and in early May, she found that she no longer had to put up with the queen and her infuriating condescension towards her. Several of Katherine's ladies, including her daughter the princess, had caught smallpox, putting them in quarantine. As a result, Henry VIII used this as an excuse to remove Anne from his wife's service and to install her in new rooms at

48. Greenwich Palace. (*By James Basire after an Unknown Artist*)

Greenwich Palace. She was relocated to the gallery by the tiltyard away from prying eyes. These lodgings, built between two great octagonal towers, formed part of a grandstand for the viewing of tournaments. Nearby was the 'disguising house' used for courtly entertainments and the banqueting hall that had welcomed the French ambassadors in the year before. This group of buildings was set apart from the palace by the royal gardens, thus affording Anne greater privacy and allowing the king to visit her discreetly as he pleased. It was there in her gallery that Anne received Edward Fox, recently returned to England. He gave her news of the 'coming of the legate … which she most thankfully received, and seemed to take the same marvellously to heart, rejoice, and comfort', as Fox wrote to Stephen Gardiner. She was so excited, he added, that she kept calling him by Gardiner's name by mistake.

As Henry and Anne waited for the arrival of the pope's representative, pestilence which Gardiner and Fox had been so worried about in Italy, appeared with 'great and furious danger' in England beginning in May. It took the form of the dreaded 'sweating sickness' which the English were no strangers to. In 1485, the epidemic had struck with a fury and then again in 1507, killing indiscriminately people of all ranks and ages: 'those that died were first attacked with a great cold, next with a fervent heat and sweating when they became delirious.' The disease was highly contagious, and those who were able fled from the centres of outbreak to isolate themselves in the country.

By June, instances of the sweat appeared at court. Among those afflicted was a servant of Anne's and because she had been in close proximity to her mistress, Anne was forced to retire to Hever Castle for the time being. But the safety of home offered her no defence to the pervasiveness of the plague;

49. Sir William Butts. (*By Hans Holbein*)

Anne too caught the sweat. Instead of rushing to be by his sweetheart's side, Henry – who had always been fearful of contagion – left court for the countryside in Essex and then Hertfordshire, where he was determined to remain until the disease was gone. The only comfort he could give Anne was to send one of his physicians, William Butts, to her along with his prayers and well wishes for her recovery. In one letter, Henry wrote that Anne being sick was 'the most unpleasant news that I could receive', and that he would 'willingly bear half of your illness in order to have you cured'. Still, he was confident she would recover soon, 'which will be a greater cordial for me than all the precious stones in the world'.

50. William Carey. (*By an Unknown Artist*)

Anne did get well, as did her father and brother who had also been stricken. But another in their family was not so fortunate. William Carey, Anne's brother-in-law, was carried off by the sweat on 22 June, leaving his grieving wife a widow with two small children to raise on her own.

* * *

After she had duly recovered, Anne, who had eclipsed her father as the most influential in their family, set about exerting her influence. Her late brother-in-law, William Carey, had a sister Eleanor who was a nun, whom the Boleyns believed would be ideal to be abbess at her convent in Wiltshire. But Wolsey had someone else in mind, the current prioress Isabel Jordan. The cardinal did some digging and unearthed scandal about Eleanor Carey's 'dissolute living'. Far from leading an exemplary life in the cloisters, she had secretly given birth to two children by two different priests, and she was now the lover of a third.

Anne was enraged by the cardinal's meddling, and she and her family did some mudslinging of their own. Isabel Jordan, a paragon of virtue according to Wolsey, was no 'able and religious woman' either. The prioress had a past of her own, claimed the Boleyns. But Wolsey, who was determined to exercise his authority over Church matters, nominated Dame Isabel nonetheless. But his game of one-upmanship with Anne put him in hot water with the king. After both women were deemed unfit, Henry VIII decided that he 'would not have had her [Isabel Jordan], nor Carey's eldest sister' as abbess. However, Wolsey still went ahead and installed his candidate. He received a furious rebuke from the king who accused him of pretending not to know what his wishes were and proceeding anyways. 'It is a double offence to do ill and colour it also,' Henry wrote in anger. But after Wolsey made his apologies – he had been overwhelmed and distracted by the sweating sickness in his household – the king was forgiving. 'Seeing the humbleness of your submission,' he said magnanimously, 'I am content to remit it, and am glad that my warnings have been lovingly accepted.' It was a lesson to Wolsey not to challenge Mistress Anne again.

Chapter 8

With the impending arrival of the papal legate, Cardinal Campeggio, Anne was sent away to Hever. Once the trial was underway, her presence would only compromise the king's case. He should appear as wanting to divorce the queen solely because of his scruples, not his passion for the Lady Anne. But despite Henry's public denials that she had anything to do with it, it was no secret he was madly in love with her. The Imperial ambassador was well aware of the fact when he reported Anne's departure to Margaret of Austria in early September. It was, as he told the archduchess, 'so that the cardinal may not find her at court on his arrival'.

What Margaret now made of Anne is unknown. The archduchess refrained from making any statement about the girl she had once known in the Netherlands, but all in all, Henry VIII's *Great Matter* was repugnant to her. Margaret remained sympathetic to her former sister-in-law Katherine, and she was dismayed by the growing tensions between her nephew Charles and the King of England. In November, when she granted Henry and Katherine's request for two jurists to be sent from Mechelen to England to help decide the case, Margaret hoped for a conclusion in Katherine's favour. The 'warmth and zeal' with which she had 'taken up the affairs of the queen', earned her Henry's enmity. When Margaret later died in 1530, he received the news with pleasure, going as far as to say with unkindness that her death 'was certainly no great loss for the world'.

51. Cardinal Lorenzo Campeggio. (*By Edward Harding*)

To the added infuriation of the Imperialists, Henry and Anne were behaving as if the divorce was a fait accompli. It was reported how 'both the king and his lady ... look upon their future marriage as certain, as if that of the queen had been actually dissolved. Preparations are already being made for the wedding'. There was added excitement for the couple when in mid-September, Campeggio reached France to take ship for England. Henry immediately dashed off a note to Hever:

> The legate, which we most desire, arrived in Paris on Sunday or Monday last past; so that I trust, by the next Monday, to hear of his arrival at Calais; and then, I trust, within a while after, to enjoy that which I have so longed for, to God's pleasure and both our comforts.

Campeggio did not land in England until 29 September, and it was not until the first week of October that he was finally in London. But instead of getting down to business right away with Henry VIII and Wolsey, Campeggio shut himself in his rooms at Bath Place, an episcopal mansion on the Strand. He had been laid low by fever and gout before leaving Paris, and his crossing of the Channel in stormy weather had been 'great toil and trouble'. Campeggio was so weak that he skipped the welcoming ceremonies staged in his honour, and instead made straightway to bed. Being so out of sight, rumours were circulated around the city that the legate had actually died.

Three days later, Campeggio was well enough to pay Henry VIII a visit at Bridewell Palace. There, he conferred with the king and Wolsey for four hours, strategizing on what to do. As Campeggio told them, Pope Clement was sympathetic to the couple and would ensure that their marriage be decided by a fair trial. Still, for the sake of peace in Christendom, it would be better if the queen voluntarily withdrew her opposition and retired to a private life – perhaps a religious one – thus allowing the king to remarry. She 'would lose nothing whatever, and as so much good would ensue, I cannot see why it should be impossible to induce her to take this course, which would be less scandalous and more secure', Campeggio believed.

But Katherine refused to be swayed. When she met the legate in private, she was adamant that she was the king's true wife and that there had been no impediment against them cohabiting. So that there was

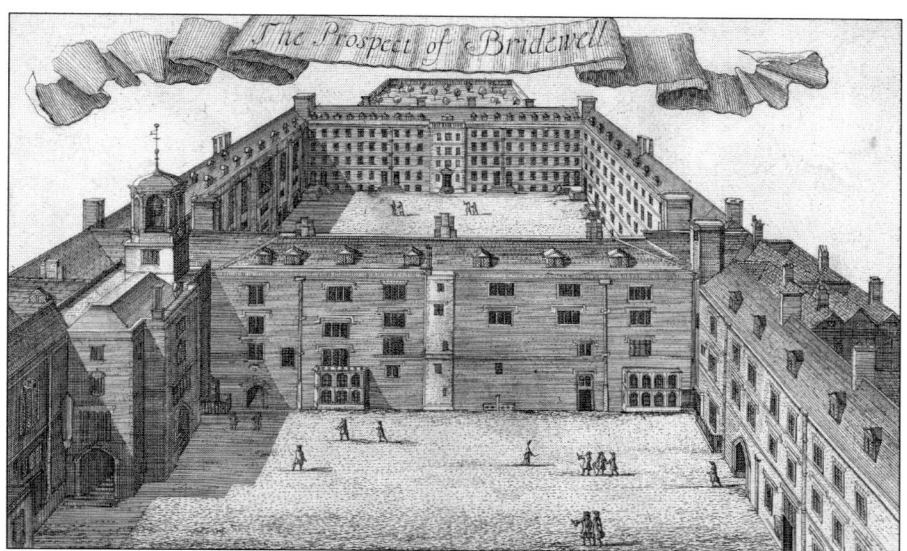

52. Bridewell Palace. (*By Johannes Kip*)

no doubt she was speaking the truth, Katherine asked Campeggio to hear her confession. The Sacrament of Reconciliation would not permit the cardinal to divulge what the queen told him, but in this instance, Katherine gave him her permission to do so at his discretion. 'For a long space' she talked about her life from her arrival in England up to her current difficulties with the king. She especially touched upon her marriage to Prince Arthur. She swore that in all the time they were together, 'she did not sleep with him more than seven nights', and that she remained 'intact and uncorrupted by him, as when she came from her the womb of her mother'. Virgin or not at the time, Campeggio nonetheless asked Katherine, in obedience to the Church, to renounce her marriage. It would preserve the tranquillity of the realm, and she would be well provided for by the king.

Katherine was dumbfounded in hearing such words from Campeggio's own lips. Sadly, neither he nor the pope had her best interests in mind and were only looking to accommodate her husband, not her. She dismissed his advice with scorn, declaring that 'she intended to live and die in the estate of matrimony, into which God had called her, and that she should always be of that opinion, and would not change it'. She was so certain of the righteousness of her cause, Katherine exclaimed, that she would rather be 'torn limb from limb' than to admit otherwise, and 'that if after death she should return to life, rather than change it, she would prefer to die over again'.

Katherine was also insistent that the pope revoke Wolsey and Campeggio's authority to try the case in England and for it to be heard in Rome instead. She would not get a fair trial, the queen claimed, as Wolsey was beholden to the king for the many benefices he had acquired over the years, and as for Campeggio, he too was in Henry VIII's pocket as the recipient of the bishopric of Salisbury. On 18 June 1529, Katherine made this appeal in open court at the Priory of the Blackfriars, but it fell upon deaf ears; her request was denied. The two cardinals promised that she would get an impartial hearing in England, and a formal summons was made for her and Henry to appear before them three days later. Katherine's only consolation was that the Bishop of Rochester, who had always been a friend and supporter of hers, would be one of her advocates at that trial.

When the proceedings began on 21 June, Katherine found herself seated across from the king, a scenario she could never have imagined having long been by his side as his wife and queen. Between them on a dais were Wolsey and Campeggio, and in the midst, were the nobles and clergy, as well as the lawyers (such as the two sent from the Netherlands) who would help decide the case. It was the king who spoke first. He made a short declaration 'to the effect that he would no longer remain in mortal sin, as he had done during the last twenty years, and that he should never be at ease until the rights of this marriage were decided'. But it was not the king's appeal that moved the audience, but the queen's. Katherine rose from her seat and made her way across the room to Henry. She fell on her knees before him, and with tears in her eyes, begged him to reconsider. Before the court, she reminded him how she had lived as his wife for many years, and 'that she did not deserve to be repudiated and thus put to shame without any cause, and she besought the said judges to show her favour'. And as for her virginity which so much of the case hung upon, Katherine again affirmed that upon their wedding day, she was 'a true maid without touch of man'. She committed her cause entirely to God, she said, and she then left the court never to return again.

Katherine was declared contumacious and the trial continued in spite of her wilful absence. Depositions were taken from those present at her wedding to Prince Arthur to determine what had really happened.

53. The Family of Henry VII at Worship. (*By Charles Grignion after an Unknown Artist*). From left: Prince Edmund, Prince Henry, Prince Arthur, King Henry, Queen Elizabeth, Princess Margaret, Princess Elizabeth, Princess Mary, and Princess Katherine.

Among those subpoenaed was Thomas Boleyn. The viscount testified that he personally believed that Arthur and Katherine had consummated their marriage as they were both old enough to. He was apparently not present for the ceremonial bedding of the couple, but the Marquess of Dorset was. He remembered seeing Arthur going to bed after his nuptials, 'where the Lady Katherine lay under the coverlet, as the manner is of queens in that behalf'. Dorset was certain that afterwards in private, the boy 'used the princess as his wife, for he was of a good and sanguine complexion, and they were commonly reputed as man and wife during Prince Arthur's life'. Sir Antony Willoughby was even more explicit. On the morning after, he recollected, the prince said to him and other witnesses, 'Willoughby, bring me a cup of ale, for I have been this night in the midst of Spain! Masters, it is good pastime to have a wife!' By his

54. The Death of Richard Hunne (from John Foxe's *Acts and Monuments*).

bawdy remark, Willoughby had no doubt that the prince and princess had had sex together. But not all the deponents were convinced. The Bishop of Ely was doubtful as the queen had always told him that she had never known her first husband carnally.

Even after all the testimonies were heard, no decision was made for or against the divorce. Campeggio had been given secret instructions from Clement VII to make no pronouncement and to refer the case to Rome. On 23 July, the day when judgment was to be rendered, the legate closed the proceedings and adjourned the court. Henry VIII, who was observing in private nearby, was livid. He ordered his brother-in-law, the Duke of Suffolk, to convey his anger to the assembly. Brandon went into the court and shouted, 'It was never merry in England whilst we had cardinals among us!' For Wolsey, it was no less than the writing on the wall for himself.

* * *

The king's disdain for churchmen like Cardinal Campeggio was shared by Anne Boleyn. Apart from her personal dislike of Wolsey, she was also contemptuous of over-mighty clergy who presumed themselves to be the equal of kings. In her youth, Anne had been taught to have an abiding respect and obedience to the Church, but in the years since, there had been a rise of anti-clericalism in England among her generation.

The long resentment came to a head in 1514 with the notorious affair of Richard Hunne. Hunne was a London merchant whose infant son had sadly died. The grief-stricken father refused to part with the boy's expensive baptismal cloth as a fee to the priest conducting the funeral, and for that, he was put into a church prison. Hunne was later found hanging in his cell, an apparent suicide. It was highly suspected that he was actually murdered, but the matter was never fully resolved.

Criticism of the Church was further incited by events from abroad. In 1517, in Germany, the monk Martin Luther publicly criticized the sale of indulgences by the Church, and he was creating extra controversy by promoting the doctrine of justification – that humankind was saved by its faith alone in Christ, not by doing good works or by the agency of the Church.

Henry VIII had found Luther's views repugnant, and in response he had written *The Defence of the Seven Sacraments*, for which he was given the title *Defender of the Faith* by a grateful Vatican in 1521. But by the time he was pursuing his divorce, Henry's regard for the authority and infallibility of the papacy was far less enthusiastic, thanks in part to the influence of Anne Boleyn. Anne was attracted to religious reform due to her acquaintance with the likeminded Margaret of Angoulême while in France. While she did adhere to certain traditional beliefs such as the sanctity of the Mass, performing good deeds for one's salvation, and the efficacy of going to confession and on pilgrimages, Anne – like her father and her brother – had an evangelical bent to her. Although she and her family were accused of being 'more Lutheran than Luther himself', and of being supportive of 'heretical doctrines and practices', these were exaggerations. What the Boleyns were interested in was in seeking a more intimate relationship with God. They were especially drawn to the active reading and studying of the Bible – particularly in the vernacular – and of other religious works, including commentaries about faith and its role in society.

In 1529, one such piece of writing came to the attention of Anne – a tract by the lawyer Simon Fish. She may have been attracted to it as she knew that the author was persona non grata to Cardinal Wolsey. At Christmas 1526, the lawyers at Gray's Inn had put on an entertainment about the governance of the kingdom being put into decay. However, none of them had dared to take on the controversial role of *Dissipation and Negligence* except Fish. Even though the play was written twenty years ago, this character was now seen to represent the unpopular Wolsey. Not surprisingly, when the cardinal learnt of the masque being performed, he ordered the arrest of the organizer of the event, John Roo, and of Fish. The latter had to flee to Germany to evade Wolsey's wrath. There he met William Tyndale, a radical English scholar, who encouraged Fish to compose a tract entitled *A Supplication for the Beggars*.

55. Martin Luther. (*By Lucas Cranach*)

Anne read it with great interest. Fish railed against the corruption of the Church and called the clergy an 'idle ravenous sort'. Such 'wolves' had enriched themselves at the expense of the king and his people, and were in ownership of a third of England's wealth. Their riches, the writer warned the king, had been extorted from his subjects by unfair fees and taxes made out to corrupt churchmen. Failure or refusal to pay resulted in charges of heresy by the priests (obviously a reference to the Richard Hunne scandal). 'Is it any marvel that your people so complain of poverty,' Fish asked the king? Not only was the clergy greedy, he wrote, but also presumptuous, wanting to 'translate all rule, power, lordship, authority, obedience, and dignity from Your Grave unto them'.

Even though *A Supplication* had been dedicated and addressed to Henry VIII, because of its unapologetic and strident anti-clericalism, it had to be smuggled into England. Anne was unsure of how the king would take it and she was hesitant to show it to him at first. But at the urging of her brother George, she finally did. To Henry it was a revelation. He devoured its contents for days, and he even invited Fish back home from his exile. Upon his return, the king 'embraced him with loving countenance', and the two talked for hours afterwards about Fish's views.

The Boleyns were responsible for introducing another radical work to the king. Fish's friend, William Tyndale, had written a book entitled *The Obedience of a Christian Man*. Like Fish's work, it was anti-clerical and it questioned the legitimacy of papal supremacy beyond the confines of Rome. A banned copy had come into Anne's possession, but before she could share it with the king, it was confiscated by Richard Sampson, the Dean of the King's Chapel. Sampson, a conservative who was siding with Queen Katherine over the *Great Matter*, was loathe that anyone, especially the king, should see it. In response, Anne went directly to Henry and complained. 'It shall be the dearest book,' she declared, 'that ever dean or cardinal took away!' Sure enough, he agreed. Tyndale's argument that the pope, being a foreigner, had no jurisdiction over the Church of England struck a chord with Henry, as did his notion that the sovereign's authority extended over matters spiritual as well as secular. 'This is a book for me and all kings to read!' he exclaimed. Its profound effect on Henry would dictate his actions to come.

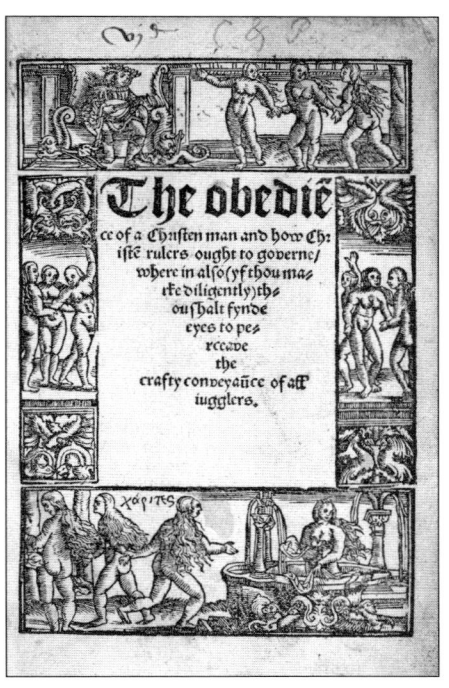

56. *The Obedience of a Christian Man.* (*By William Tyndale*)

Part III

'Lady Anne, considering herself already sure of her affair, is fiercer than a lioness.'

Eustace Chapuys to Charles V, 1531

Chapter 9

Wolsey was mortified by Campeggio's suspension of the trial at Blackfriars. But as the legate reassured him, it was merely a summer break following Italian custom; the proceedings would recommence in the autumn, on 1 October. However, the day came and went, and on the 5th, Campeggio left England for good. The truth was that Pope Clement had revoked the powers of the two cardinals and referred the case to the Roman courts. Wolsey had failed his master, and he could expect the worst to come.

Perhaps the king, remembering his past service to him, would be forgiving, but what about Mistress Anne? Since becoming Henry's beloved, she was queen in all but name. 'Greater court is now paid to *her* every day,' said the French ambassador, than there had been to Katherine of Aragon for a long while. Wolsey knew how Anne could be quick to anger, and certainly, she would blame *him* for preventing her marriage. As he wrote to his friend Thomas Cromwell, all would be better 'if the displeasure of my Lady Anne be somewhat assuaged as I pray God the same to be'.

But Anne was determined to bring down the cardinal. The king had lost his trust in him and with Wolsey so vulnerable, she was ready to strike. Anne was not alone wishing him gone. Powerful men, like her father, her uncle Norfolk, and the Duke of Suffolk, had long nursed grudges against Wolsey,

57. Thomas Howard, Third Duke of Norfolk. (*By Lucas Vorsterman after Hans Holbein*)

and they were determined 'to undermine his influence with the king, and get the administration of affairs in their own hands'. Together, they whispered to Henry VIII how the proud and arrogant statesman had betrayed him and that he was unfit for office. Their efforts paid off. On 18 October – the feast day of Saint Luke the Evangelist – Wolsey himself was 'disevangelised', as it was wryly put. He was formally charged with *praemunire*, that is asserting the authority of Rome over that of the king. The accusation was absurd as Wolsey, made papal legate since 1518, was merely exercising his powers on behalf of his master, notably in the matter of his divorce.

Still, Wolsey put up no defence and admitted to the indictment. 'With bitter complaints, tears, and sighs', he surrendered his seat on the Royal Council and his prestigious title of Lord Chancellor of England. The latter was given to Sir Thomas More, the esteemed lawyer and the author of *Utopia*, 'held for his uprightness of character' and 'considered the most learned man in the kingdom'. Wolsey also yielded the great riches he had accumulated over the years in hopes of appeasing Henry VIII. He gave up his palaces of York Place (to be renamed 'the King's Manor of Westminster' and then more commonly as 'Whitehall') and Hampton Court. After Wolsey went into exile to Esher, Henry and Anne – with her mother in tow as their chaperone – went to Whitehall and inspected the treasures –

58. Sir Thomas More. (*After Hans Holbein*)

jewels, tapestries, furniture, plate, and so forth – that the cardinal had left behind. Their value was of 'no trifling matter', and the king was 'much gratified and found the present more valuable even than he expected'.

But even in banishment, Wolsey – now only Archbishop of York – was still hopeful of mercy. When he fell ill in Esher, Henry VIII sent his own physician to him, and he even persuaded Anne to forward a jewel of hers as a token of her goodwill. But upon his recovery, Wolsey's optimism was shattered. On 4 November 1530, he was charged with high treason. He was accused of conspiring with the pope to prevent the annulment of the king's marriage. The cardinal was arrested by Henry Percy (now Earl of Northumberland) no less, with the intention of taking him to the Tower of London. Wolsey was certain his end was near as a divination was once given to him that he would die on his way to London. But he was spared the ignominies of a trial and undoubtedly his execution to follow. On the road to the city, the cardinal – now mortally ill – stopped at Leicester Abbey, and muttering how if he had served God as well as he did the king, the Almighty would not have abandoned him in his 'grey hairs'. He died shortly afterwards on 29 November.

* * *

Since her appearance at Blackfriars, the queen had become even more despondent, being 'very sad and disconsolate'. 'Instead of calming her husband's irritation against her', it was reported that 'she has rather increased it' by her impassioned plea to Henry in open court. Katherine continued to seek her nephew Charles's help. As always, he promised to do what he could for her and to look after her interests. He also appointed a new ambassador, Eustace Chapuys, to the English court. 'Monsieur Chapuys, officer of Geneva and of my council,' the emperor wrote,

> has been instructed by me to make every effort to persuade the king, my good brother, to keep his mind at rest, and cast away the doubts and scruples he has hitherto entertained, and may still entertain, respecting your marriage.

When Chapuys arrived in England in August 1529, Katherine found the representative to be everything she hoped for. He was intelligent,

59. Eustace Chapuys. (*By an Unknown Artist*)

assiduous, and completely devoted to her cause. In the years to come, Chapuys would go above and beyond to serve Katherine as her 'especial friend' as she came to call him, and to even put himself in danger for her sake by inciting treason against Henry VIII.

Even with their relationship under terrible strain, Henry and Katherine were still obliged to live together, if not as man and wife, then at least as king and queen. On ceremonial occasions, they still sat side by side and presided over court, much to Anne Boleyn's annoyance. No matter how 'very hault and stout' she was, 'having all manner of jewels or rich apparel that might be gotten with money', she was still merely 'the lady' or 'the concubine' as Chapuys contemptuously mocked her.

To Anne's further frustration, the king would sometimes dine with the queen. Such evenings often ended in arguments between the royal couple, but for form's sake, Henry continued to keep company with his wife. On one such occasion, Katherine was especially distraught. She was 'suffering the pains of purgatory on earth,' she cried, and 'was very badly treated' by Henry's avoidance of her. The king replied that she had no reason to complain as she could do as she pleased in her own house, and as for his frequent absences, he had affairs of state to attend to. Lastly, he was *not* her husband as she kept insisting, as many learned men, including her own almoner, were of that opinion. 'I care not a straw!' Katherine answered in a rage. 'He is not my judge in the present case. It is for the pope, not for him, to decide!' And for every one man that Henry presented for his case, she added, she could bring a thousand!

Tired of arguing with Katherine, Henry left her to her own and went to eat with Anne instead. But instead of a sympathetic ear, he got a tongue lashing from her as well. Anne, who thought that the queen was much better when it came to making arguments, did not hold back and told Henry so to his face. In the same breath, she also voiced her resentment of being still yet unmarried:

> Did I not tell you that whenever you disputed with the queen, she was sure to have the upper hand? I see that some fine morning you will succumb to her reasoning, and that you will cast me off. I have been waiting long, and might in the meanwhile have contracted some advantageous marriage, out of which I might have had issue, which is the greatest consolation in this world; but alas! Farewell to my time and youth spent to no purpose at all!

Katherine's continuing popularity was another thorn in Anne's side. Whenever she stepped out, there were crowds of people, particularly women, who cheered her on, shouting words of support and encouragement. The queen had always been well loved, and it was an affront to them that she should be so callously put away. If the King of England himself had no regard for the sanctity of marriage, what is to say that their own husbands would not take it in their heads to discard them as well and take up with another?

When she was at court, Anne was well aware of the looks and sniggers directed at her by those loyal to the queen, especially her servants. Some of them had come with Katherine from Spain, and believing that Anne had 'so enticed the king and brought him in such amours, that only for her sake and occasion, he would divorce from the queen', they had no kind words for this notorious woman. Anne retaliated in kind, saying aloud how she 'wished all the Spaniards were at the bottom of the sea' and that she would 'rather see her [Katherine] hanged than have to confess that she' was her 'queen and mistress!' And to show how little she cared what the world thought of her, Anne adopted a motto – *Ainsi sera groingné qui groingne!* (*Let those who would grumble do so!*).

Anne did not give up hope to be queen. Among those lately recruited to Henry VIII's service was an obscure cleric named Thomas Cranmer. He was an old acquaintance of Edward Fox and Stephen Gardiner, and during a chance meeting with them, Cranmer suggested a different approach to resolving the king's *Great Matter*. Rather than having it decided by an ecclesiastical court, he proposed, it ought to be put 'unto the best learned men' in the universities. When Fox and Gardiner mentioned Cranmer's novel idea to their master, Henry was impressed. 'I perceive that the man hath the sow by the right ear!' he exclaimed excitedly. The soft-spoken Cranmer was

60. Thomas Cranmer, Archbishop of Canterbury. (*By William Holl after Gerlach Flicke*)

immediately summoned to court and put to work canvassing the opinions of theologians.

Another new servant of the king was Thomas Cromwell. A former protégé of Wolsey, Cromwell, who had also come from a humble background like the late cardinal, spent his younger years as a self-described 'ruffian' upon the Continent. He supposedly served as a mercenary soldier with the French, and then later attached himself to a rich merchant in Italy. After his return to England, Cromwell, with his skill in foreign languages and his ability to get things done no matter how great the challenges, attracted the attention of Wolsey. He worked as a lawyer for the cardinal, and when he fell from power, Cromwell was said to be much affected. In tears, he lamented how he too had come to misfortune 'for doing of my master true and diligent service' and being tied to him. But determined to start anew, Cromwell went into royal service and in time became truly indispensable to Henry VIII.

Cromwell was able to convince his new master to truly assert his powers. Thomas More would later advise and warn him, that to be a 'true faithful servant and a right worthy councillor' to the king, he must always 'tell him what he ought to do, but never what he is able to do … for if a lion knew his own strength, hard were it for any man to rule him'. But to Cromwell, the sovereign was not a man to be reined in and managed, but given his full authority to exercise his might. To achieve that end, Cromwell worked up an extraordinary charge against the Church of England. In December 1530, the entire clergy was accused of *praemunire*, the same indictment that brought down Cardinal Wolsey. For accepting the pope's authority over the monarch's, the Lords Spiritual were called to the Court of the King's Bench to answer for their offence. Remembering the fate of Wolsey, the day before their appearance in court, the churchmen submitted themselves to the king's mercy and offered him £100,000 (about £44 million today) in contrition. Henry VIII willingly accepted the 'gift' and gave them his pardon, but not without another concession. All those in holy orders had to renounce their allegiance to the pope and recognize him as 'Supreme Head of the Church in England'.

Even with the clergy kowtowing to the king, Queen Katherine refused to budge from her position. Not even the opinions of the universities collected by Thomas Cranmer could change her mind. Some of them had found in the king's favour, declaring that 'neither by the law of God, nor of nature' could a man take his brother's widow as his wife even with a dispensation from the pope. On 31 May 1531, these findings – those to the contrary having been suppressed of course – were presented to Katherine. But when she was told how 'a great number of clerks and well learned men had determined the king's marriage to be unlawful, detestable, and against God's law', she would still not back down. Her father, King Ferdinand, Katherine responded, had himself consulted with many wise men before he – not to mention King Henry VII as well – assented to her being the wife of her brother-in-law. And as for the judgment of the universities, she was 'but a woman and lack wit and leaning to answer them,' Katherine continued, thereby she committed her case entirely to God.

61. Thomas Cromwell. (*By an Unknown Artist*)

The queen's stubbornness and her self-righteousness only increased Anne Boleyn's hatred of her. If not for Katherine, she would have long ago married the king, and with her being a continuing presence in their lives, there was no end in sight, Anne fumed. Under great strain, she became difficult and picked fights with the king's servants. They were either for or against her, and courtiers, such as Sir Henry Guildford,

62. Sir Henry Guildford. (*By Wenceslaus Hollar after Hans Holbein*)

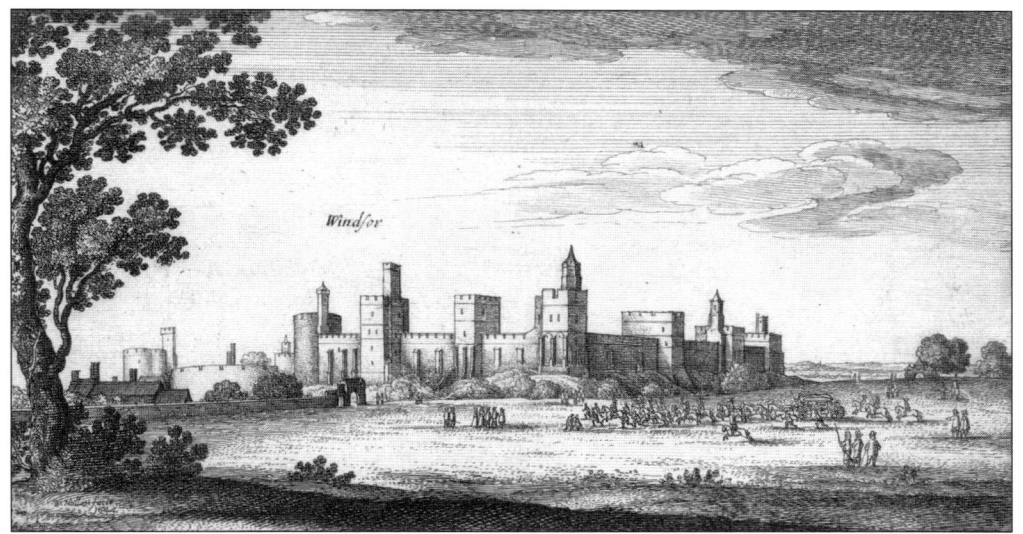

63. Windsor Castle. (*By Wenceslaus Hollar*)

did not escape her sharp tongue. An old favourite of Henry VIII and the comptroller of his household, Guildford made no secret of his loyalty to Katherine of Aragon. Anne confronted him one day, saying that when she becomes queen, she will have him 'punished and deprived of his office'. Guildford refused to bow and scrape to the king's mistress, and he told Anne directly that should that happen, he would quit his post and save her the trouble.

Anne even fought with the king. The pair had become such a *cause célèbre* throughout Europe that gossip about them even reached Rome. To the amusement of Pope Clement, he had heard that the mighty King of England had been reduced to begging Anne's relatives – with tears in his eyes no less – 'to try and adjust the difference between them'. In his passion for the lady 'whose will is law to him', he had been become a figure of international ridicule.

Perhaps it was at Anne's urging that Henry finally cut his ties to Katherine of Aragon. That summer, the court had moved from Greenwich to Windsor Castle, and on 14 July, without a word of goodbye to his wife, Henry – with Anne by his side on a hunting trip – left Windsor never to see her again.

Chapter 10

When the king and his court returned to Windsor in August, Anne was exhilarated. Katherine was gone for good, having been expelled and ordered to take up residence at The More in Hertfordshire, once owned by Cardinal Wolsey. While nothing remains of it today, it was once a fine palace, so much so that a French envoy thought more highly of it than Hampton Court. Amidst its splendour, Katherine ruled over her court-in-exile. By all appearances, she was still queen and treated as such. She was given 200 persons to wait upon her, and when she dined in public, she was served by fifty butlers, while thirty maids-of-honour stood by. Such displays were important to Katherine as to give the impression that she was still the king's true wife. Those who saw her at The More said she always had 'a smile on her countenance', but in actuality, Katherine was doing her best to hide the pain of her abandonment. After Henry had left her, she had sent a letter to him asking after him. In reply, she received a stinging message telling her that he did not care for her well wishes, and that 'she had hitherto caused him

64. A View of Hampton Court as Finished by K. Henry VIII. (*By John Pye after Wenceslaus Hollar*)

much annoyance and sorrow in a thousand ways'. He was particularly angry that she had referred their case to Rome, and to his dishonour, he had been summoned to appear in person to defend himself.

With Katherine in banishment, a delighted Anne, 'as if she were already a queen', took over the royal apartments at Greenwich Palace. She was also given new rooms at Whitehall. Since his takeover of it from Wolsey, Henry VIII had thought it too small for his needs and was intent on enlarging it as his London seat. Thomas Cromwell, now a member of the king's Privy Council, was assigned to buy up properties south of the palace. These were then razed to the ground and the land used for the new extensions. A 'queen's side' was constructed for Anne, along with a house in the nearby park. The latter was intended for the future Prince of Wales, the son she and Henry would surely have. There were also plans to expand Hampton Court. A new section would be made for Anne on its eastern side, complete with a new courtyard. During the progress of the new constructions, Anne, with her awareness of the lavish buildings she had seen in the Low Countries and in France, had her say in their designs and layouts.

Anne's determination to be queen and to bear the king a proper heir was the subject of an unusual tale from around this time. As related by George Wyatt, she had stumbled across a book of prophecies one day giving her dire warning of things to come. In it, were a king marked *H*, a queen in mourning called *K*, and a woman with her head off as *A*. When Anne showed it to her servant named Nan, the girl was horrified. 'If I thought it true,' she said, 'though he were an emperor, I would not myself marry him with that condition!' If the book was meant to frighten Anne, it failed as it only made her more determined. 'I think the book a bauble,' she said resolutely. 'Yet for the hope I have that the realm may be happy by my issue, I am resolved to have him whatsoever might become of me.'

* * *

On the early morning of 11 October 1532, hours before sunrise, the docks at Dover were bustling. The royal ship, *The Swallow*, was being prepared and loaded for a voyage across the Channel. Weeks earlier, letters had been sent out by Henry VIII to his 'nobility, prelates and servants, commanding them to be ready ... to pass the seas with him for the accomplishing of the interview between him and his brother the French king'. Among the nobles going to Calais were the Dukes of Richmond, Norfolk, and Suffolk, six earls including Thomas Boleyn (made Earl of Wiltshire at the end of 1529), and several viscounts, one of which was George Boleyn who had been elevated to Lord Rochford when his father received his earldom. There were also two marquesses coming along, one of them the king's cousin, Henry Courtenay, and the other Anne Boleyn.

A month earlier, at a unique ceremony at Windsor Castle, Anne, dressed in 'a surcoat of crimson velvet, furred with ermines, with strait sleeves' and 'completely covered with the most costly jewels' was brought before the king. She knelt before him while Stephen Gardiner (now Bishop of Winchester) read out a patent creating her Marquess – not 'Marchioness' as the female equivalent was – of Pembroke in her own right with lands yielding an annual revenue of £1,000 (about £441,000 today). The king then placed a mantle about Anne's shoulders and a coronet upon her head, her hair being worn long and loose for the occasion. If Anne could not yet

65. Calais in the 16th Century. (*By an Unknown Artist*)

be a royal, she could least be an aristocrat for the upcoming meeting with the King of France.

Confident of Francis's support, Henry and Anne expected to be married very soon. 'As if she were already a queen', Anne had demanded Katherine's jewels to wear to Calais. Although she had a treasure trove of her own given to her by the king, she would not be satisfied until she laid hands upon her rival's. When the request was made to Katherine, she was outraged. Out of charity, she usually made no comment against Mistress Anne, but this time her audacity was too much to take. She absolutely refused. Katherine told the messenger, it would much distress her conscience were she to deliver up her 'jewels for so bad a purpose as that of decorating a woman who was a scandal to the whole of Christendom, and a cause of infamy to the king'. Anne has often been blamed for the mistreatment of Katherine of Aragon, but in truth, Henry VIII did not stand sheepishly by allowing Anne to act alone. However domineering Anne could be, he was equally involved in the bullying of his wife. When Katherine was finally made to give up her jewels by his direct order, Henry was reported as being 'exceedingly pleased and happy'.

Besides the loss of her valuables, Katherine was also distressed by rumours that Henry and Anne were intending to marry in Calais. But as Eustace Chapuys reassured her, Anne had no intention of being wed overseas, but in the heart of Westminster Abbey. Even if the king insisted, she was heard to say, 'she would never consent to the marriage taking place out of England, but only on the very spot and with the same ceremonies used by the English queens at their marriage and coronation'. There was also speculation that the Tower of London, which was being restored that autumn, was meant to serve as the queen's prison while Henry and Anne were away. That was untrue. The repairs were in anticipation of receiving another queen – Queen Anne – so sure was the king that the divorce would soon be realized with French help.

When Henry and Anne reached Calais, it was the king alone who went ahead to Boulogne to see Francis I. Originally, Anne, as the new Marquess of Pembroke, was to be by her lover's side in the meetings with the French; however, she was forced to stay behind. Protocol required that she be received by a great lady, but none was satisfactory to Henry VIII. Queen Claude had died in 1524, and Francis's current wife, Eleanor of Austria, whom Anne had formerly known in the Netherlands, was

66. Eleanor of Austria, Queen of France. (*By Cornelis Anthonisz*)

unacceptable as she was Katherine of Aragon's niece. A certain Madame de Vendôme was equally objectionable. She was a high-ranking member of the French court, but 'of doubtful company' having led a life of ill repute, it was said. The one person Anne truly wanted to see was Margaret of Angoulême, but she was reported to be indisposed.

Anne did not show herself until 27 October. Since she was unable to see King Francis beforehand, she was determined to make an impression upon him when she did. No expense had been spared by Henry and Anne for their trip abroad. To meet their costs for the three weeks' stay, Thomas Cromwell, as 'Master of the King's Jewels and one of his most honorable Council', was ordered to provide them with £2,000, and from his vice-treasurer of Calais, the king demanded an additional £3,000 (about £2.2 million in total today).

Anne arranged for Staple Hall in Calais, where the two kings were to dine that night, to be beautifully decorated. The banqueting chamber was hung with cloth-of-gold and cloth-of-silver, and it was lit by an abundance of candles supported by branches of silver and gilt held to the walls by chains. The showpiece of the room was a great cupboard, seven stages high, stacked with solid gold plate (mere gilt would not do). The interior of Staple Hall was so gleaming that 'there was nothing occupied that night, but all of gold'.

After the two kings and their guests had supper, Anne, and a band of attendants, which included her sister Mary and her sister-in-law, Jane Parker, Lady Rochford (married to George Boleyn in about 1525), came into the hall disguised 'in masking apparel of strange fashion, made of cloth-of-gold'. Each selected a partner for the dance, with Anne picking the French king. During the merriment, a playful Henry VIII went about removing the ladies' masks, and Francis found that he had been chosen by Mistress Anne. Afterwards, the two talked in private together. Almost certainly, Anne spoke of her fond memories of her time with Queen Claude, and how grateful she was that Francis was now lending his support to her marriage. It was in this assurance that as they waited for a fair wind back to England, Henry and Anne probably began consummating their love at long last.

Chapter 11

At dawn on 25 January 1533, Henry VIII and Anne Boleyn, with only three servants between them, convened in a private room above the gatehouse at Whitehall. The earliness of the day and the small number of attendants signified the need for secrecy for what was about to take place. Henry Norris and Thomas Heneage of the royal Privy Chamber, and Anne Savage, a lady-in-waiting, were to be the sole witnesses to Henry and Anne's marriage. Their recent sexually intimacy had resulted in the inevitable: Anne was pregnant. For the child – unquestionably a son – to be born legitimate, she and the king must be made husband and wife in the eyes of God. The officiant was either one of the royal chaplains, Rowland Lee, or an obscure friar from the Order of Saint Augustine named George Brown.

The priest and the three attendants had all been sworn to secrecy, but the couple themselves could not help but drop hints as to what had occurred. In the middle of February, Anne brazenly told her uncle, the Duke of Norfolk, and others within earshot, that if she was still not pregnant after Easter, she would go on a pilgrimage to the Shrine of Our Lady of Walsingham. Revered for centuries as the site where the Virgin Mary had supposedly made a miraculous appearance, it was a fashionable place of devotion attracting both high and low. Many of Henry VIII's royal predecessors had visited the shrine, and he himself went in 1511 in thanksgiving for his short-lived son.

In her excitement and joy, Anne also intimated that she was a married woman and much more to her old admirer Thomas Wyatt. She had a felt such a violent desire to eat apples as she had never felt before, she told him. This must surely be a sign that she was with child as the king said to her. Anne teasingly assured Wyatt she was not, and she then broke out in peals of laughter and departed, leaving him and the others present in astonishment. Henry was just as bad in keeping a secret. At a dinner party, he pointed out a cupboard filled with rich plate worth £1,188

67. The Marriage of Henry VIII and Anne Boleyn. (*By Christian Gottlieb Geyser after Daniel Nikolaus Chodowiecki*)

68. The Ruins of Walsingham Abbey in the 18th Century. (*By Gerard Vandergucht after J. Badslade in* Vetusta Monumenta)

(about £524,200 today) he had given Anne when the two of them visited the Jewel House in the Tower of London in December. As he did so, he asked her step-grandmother, the Dowager Duchess of Norfolk, who was seated next to him, didn't the Marquess of Pembroke have a 'fine dowry and a rich marriage portion'?

Come Easter Saturday, there was no more mystery. That morning, Anne – no more the Marquess of Pembroke but the Queen of England – processed to Mass 'in truly royal state, loaded with diamonds and other precious stones, and dressed in a gorgeous suit of tissue'. Her train was held by her cousin, Lady Mary Howard, and she was accompanied by a large suite of ladies, much greater in number, it was noticed, than Katherine of Aragon ever had. During the service, Anne was prayed for as queen, and afterwards, the nobles, at the king's command, were made to pay their respects to her. It was all so incredible, Chapuys wrote the emperor, that it seemed unreal, and one did not know 'whether to laugh or cry at it'.

For those who remained devoted to Katherine of Aragon and took Anne Boleyn as nothing more than a scheming supplanter, there was further grief in the weeks to come. On 23 May, Thomas Cranmer, the recently consecrated Archbishop of Canterbury, replacing the late William Warham, pronounced in Henry VIII's favour at last. 'The matrimony between the king and the Lady Katherine [was] dissolved by sufficient authority,' and Anne was recognized as his one and only true wife. When

Katherine was told, she was astounded, but she stood her ground as she always did. As long as she lived, she would entitle herself queen, she said, and if the king were to deprive her of all she had, she would 'willingly go about the world begging alms for the love of God'. And as for the pope, to prevent him from meddling and doing mischief to the king, Cranmer and his ecclesiastical court declared that the Vatican had no power to excommunicate Henry for his actions, and that it must simply accept 'what is done cannot be undone'.

Anne had thought herself cheated of a great wedding at Westminster Abbey, but she was determined to make up for it at her coronation. On the afternoon of 29 May, a vast flotilla of barges – all richly decorated with banners and pennants denoting their occupants – was seen before the Palace of Greenwich awaiting the new Queen of England. At the king's instruction, the lords spiritual and temporal, the city officials, and the representatives of the guilds were to accompany his wife in a great river pageant to the Tower of London, where, following tradition, she would rest before her crowning.

69. Lady Mary Howard, Later Duchess of Richmond and Somerset. (*By Francesco Bartolozzi after Hans Holbein*)

In readiness for her triumph, Anne had chosen a special barge for herself – the one belonging to the deposed Katherine. At her command, the ex-queen's coat of arms was hacked off of it and replaced by her own. All that was Katherine's was now hers. Dressed in cloth-of-gold, Anne sailed leisurely upon the Thames with her

70. Anne Boleyn's Device of the White Falcon. (*By an Unknown Artist*)

ladies. She was given an escort worthy of her new royal state. The Lord Mayor and the city companies rode along in fifty barges, while various nobles, including Thomas Boleyn and the Duke of Suffolk, sat in their own – each ship 'decked with innumerable banners and all about hanged with rich cloth-of-gold', and carrying minstrels 'making great and sweet harmony'. In contrast to their melodious notes were the savage cries of performers dressed up as monstrous 'wild men' to entertain the onlookers who had piled onto the riverbanks to watch the procession. They danced about their boat and threw fireballs into the river while a giant mechanical dragon behind them blew out flames from its nostrils. Anne was undoubtedly delighted by this show, but what probably gave her even more pleasure was a barge seen alongside the mayor's. On top of it was her device – a white falcon wearing a crown and clutching a sceptre, and standing proudly upon a stump from which the red roses of Lancaster and the white roses of York sprang forth.

When the procession – some 300 vessels – came in sight of Limehouse and Ratcliff, shots of ordnance were fired in salute of the new queen, and then more when Anne landed at Tower Wharf. She was received by Sir Edmund Walsingham and Sir William Kingston, the Lieutenant of the Tower and the Constable of the Tower respectively, who cleared a path to the drawbridge leading into the great fortress. There by the court gate of the Byward Tower was Henry VIII. With 'great reverence and a joyful countenance', he greeted his wife with a kiss and he placed his hands upon her belly, drawing the crowd's attention to her pregnant state. True to her new motto, Anne was indeed *The Most Happy*.

The Tower of London, in which the royal couple took up residence for the next two days, had been refurbished at great expense. Under Thomas Cromwell's supervision, several buildings were fixed up and redecorated. The Great Hall where Henry and Anne dined with their guests was repaired, and a 'queen's great chamber' was made within. In the inmost ward where the palace complex was situated, much new work had been required as the royal lodgings had fallen into neglect and were reported as being 'wonderous foul'; the king had not stayed there since his own crowning in 1509. A new wing was created for Anne, while the roofs and floors of some older apartments were given an overhaul, along with the dining chamber. The windows were also redone, giving Anne magnificent views of the garden on the east side. Although the

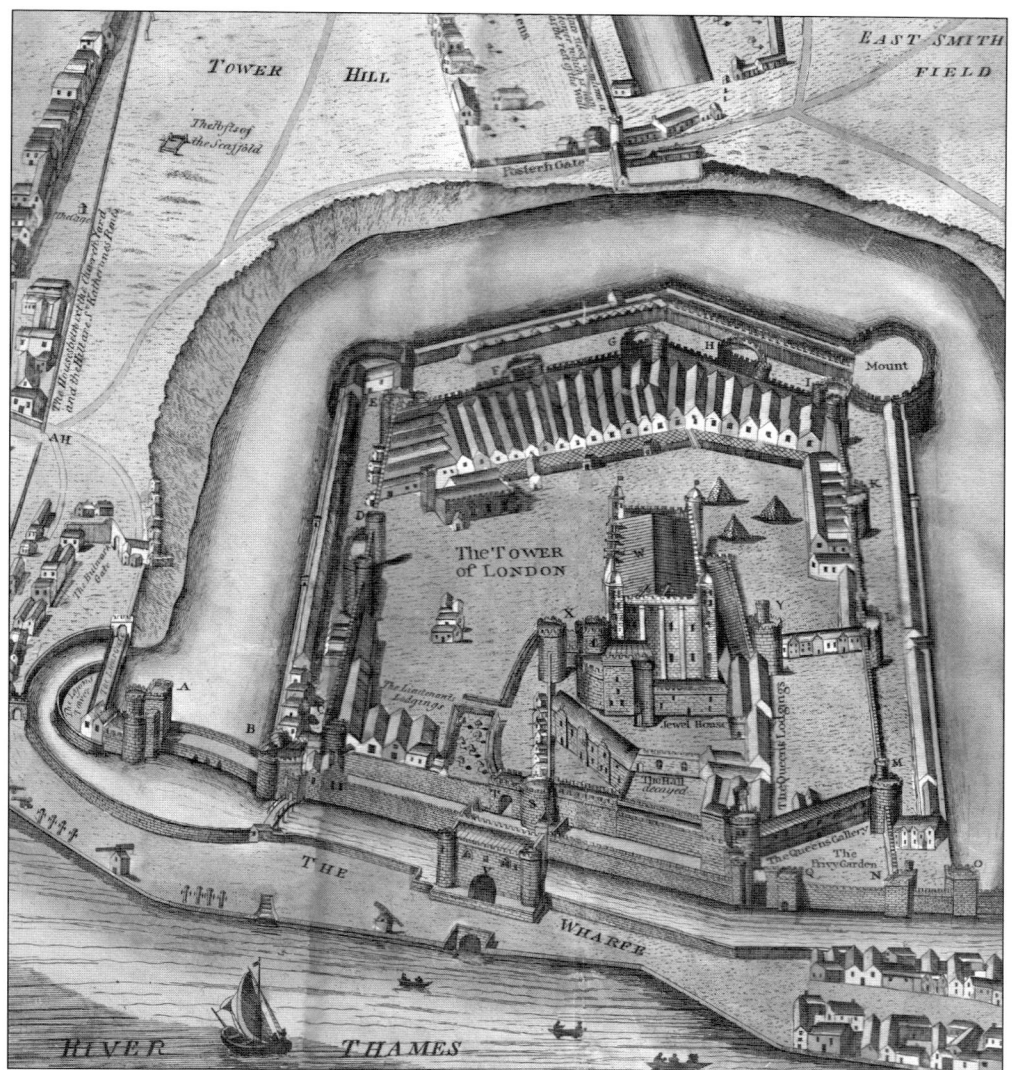

71. The Tower of London, detail. (*After William Haiward and John Gascoyne, 1597*)

king had his own rooms in and around the Lanthorn Tower along the inner curtain wall, he was given access to his wife's chambers by a special key which could open the locks to Anne's quarters.

Beyond the confines of the royal palace, the White Tower – the great central keep – was looked to as well. Domed cupolas – still in place today – were set up upon the four corner turrets, and the whole structure was a given a new coat of gleaming white paint in anticipation of the coronation. Even the bridge at the Lions' Tower (used as a zoo to house the king's collection of exotic creatures) at the western end of the citadel was mended. The queen was to set out from here into the city in full view of the people, and it needed to look its best.

In the late afternoon of 31 May – Whitsunday Eve – Anne was seen in public at last. From the Lions' Tower barbican, amidst the roars of the caged beasts nearby, she came out in a litter covered in white satin and drawn by two white horses. Anne herself was all in white as well, dressed in 'the same fashion as those of France'. Following the custom of the crowning of queens, she wore her long dark hair loose over her shoulders and upon her head was an open crown studded with precious stones. The procession did not get underway until 5 o'clock in the afternoon, perhaps to avoid the heat of the sun. To ensure Anne's comfort and in keeping with her regal state, a canopy was held above her by the Barons of the Cinque Ports all along the way to Westminster.

A number of foreign envoys, especially from France, were noticed in the parade. The Frenchmen were preeminent in recognition of King Francis's approval of Henry VIII's new marriage, and such merchants were seen wearing the new queen's heraldic colours upon their sleeves. Needless to say, there were no representatives from Emperor Charles. Behind Anne herself was a large retinue of ladies, which included her mother sitting in a chariot with the old Dowager Duchess of Norfolk. Other women – among them Mary Boleyn and Lady Rochford – followed in carriages and on horseback. A notable absentee was the Duchess of Suffolk. Mary Tudor was devoted to her sister-in-law Katherine, and she snubbed Anne by refusing to attend her coronation. Apart from her ill feelings towards her new sister-in-law, there was another reason why Mary was not seen. She was gravely ill, and in less than a month, she would be dead.

Throughout the city, fountains gushed forth with wine for the citizens, and numerous pageants were erected in tribute to Queen Anne. Most impressive was a tableau designed by Hans Holbein depicting the Greek god Apollo and the Nine Muses atop Mount Parnassus. As Anne approached, she was saluted with 'many goodly verses to her great praise and honour'. Other presentations incorporated settings from classical mythology too, but the Bible was prominent as well. At one stop, children playing the parts of Saint Anne and her family, welcomed her namesake to the city and compared her future offspring to the likes of Christ and

72. Westminster Abbey. (*By Wenceslaus Hollar*)

the apostles James and John. That the queen's own child would be born to greatness was further emphasized at another pageant. At a staging where 'sat three fair ladies, virgins, costly arrayed', one of them held a long scroll upon which was written: 'Queen Anne, when thou shalt bear a new son of the king's blood, there shall be a golden world unto thy people!' It was in this hope on the following day, Whitsunday, that Anne 'received her crown, with all the ceremonies thereof' in Westminster Abbey.

* * *

In the weeks following Anne's triumph, a great comet was seen blazing across the skies of London. Looking like 'a star with a mane like a horse's tail' ten yards long and 'traversing the Milky Way', it was also observed in Italy and even in the Far East. Such phenomena were usually interpreted as harbingers of destruction to princes. In 1066, a star 'trailing its extended and fiery train along the sky' was said to have foretold ruin to King Harold of England and to the Byzantine emperor Constantine X.

A comet had likewise appeared in October 1532. To the Romans, it had signified doom: the impending death of Pope Clement VII and fear of another invasion by Charles V. Even the English had seen it as an omen. As the king and his mistress were preparing to take ship to Calais, a star 'in the form of a luminous silver beard' appeared in the heavens, along with other 'prodigies'. 'A dead fish of marvellous size, ninety feet long' was cast ashore in the north, and at the Palace of Greenwich, the tide had flowed for nine hours straight and overspilled the riverbank to reach the very walls of the chapel, 'a thing never hitherto seen or heard of'. At the same time, Elizabeth Barton, the celebrated 'Nun of Kent' who was given to ecstatic visions of heaven and hell, foretold that Anne would come to 'great shame' should she wed the king. But these so-called portents had meant nothing to Henry and Anne the year before, and the new comet coming into sight did not shake their confidence about their continuing happiness. As William Kingston wrote to his friend Lord Lisle in the summer of 1533, the king and his new queen were 'well and merry' and 'Her Grace has a fair belly as I have seen'.

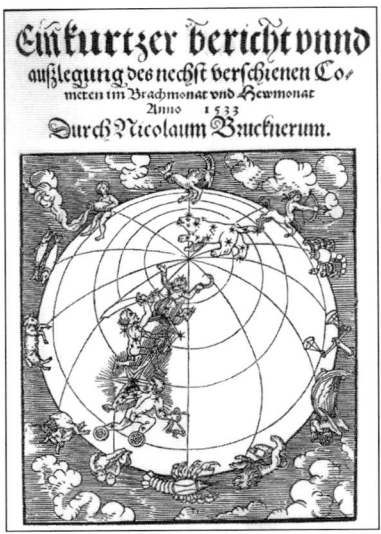

73. The Great Comet of 1533. (*By Nicolaus Prueckner*) It is seen passing through the constellations of Auriga, Perseus, and Cassiopeia towards the Great Bear.

Since her coronation, 'pastime in the queen's chamber was never more' with much reverie by Anne's ladies. If any gentleman attached to them thought himself missed in being absent from court, the Lord Chamberlain told George Boleyn, he would be sadly mistaken by all the gaiety surrounding the queen. Anne herself was still in euphoria, with her happiness even transcending the earthly. When the Venetian ambassador came to offer her his congratulations, Anne was assured that her good fortune was preordained and blessed by Heaven. She knew that God had inspired His Majesty to marry her, she said to him confidently.

The king too was convinced that his marriage was divinely decreed. He had no doubt that the child Anne was carrying was a boy. All the doctors and the astrologers he had consulted had assured him of the fact. In expectation of the prince's birth, Henry planned a great pageant and tournament in the baby's honour, and he sent agents to Flanders to buy horses for the big day. He even arranged to have the prince delivered in the greatest finery. 'One of the most magnificent and gorgeous beds that could be thought of' – so much so that it was part of a ransom of a French duke – was taken from the royal treasure house and installed at Greenwich. According to Eustace Chapuys who hated Anne even more now that she had displaced the former queen, she ought to be satisfied as she and Henry VIII had fought recently. During her pregnancy, the king distracted himself with a flirtation with a lady of the court, and Anne, in great jealousy, made a scene.

In the past, Henry had never dared to contradict her; so much so that that it was joked about how henpecked he was and how his court was in disorder because of that. The news from abroad told how 'the king is abused by the new queen, and that his gentlemen goeth daily a playing where they woll, and His Grace abides by her all the day long, and dare not go out for the rumour of the people'. While Henry did allow himself to be ruled by Anne during their long courtship, by the time they married, the dynamic of their relationship had changed. Anne was now expected to be subservient and submissive – even when it came to matters of sex. If he wished to take mistresses, Henry told her bluntly, she must be as tolerant as Katherine of Aragon had been. But Anne refused to play second fiddle. She raged against her husband making 'use of certain words which he very much disliked'. In turn, Henry warned Anne to 'shut her eyes and endure as those who were better than herself had done, and that she ought to know that he could at any time, lower her as much as he had raised her'.

While this incident might have given hope to Katherine and her supporters that the couple's relationship was souring, Chapuys was more realistic. Despite the king and queen not speaking to each other for two or three days afterwards, he noted that it was merely a lovers' quarrel of which 'no great notice should be taken'. Nonetheless, the envoy confided to the emperor, knowing the king's capriciousness, it was not impossible that he would eventually tire of Anne and even take back his former wife.

But that hope seemed increasingly remote when Anne went into seclusion at Greenwich to await childbirth. At the end of August, she took her leave of the court, and with her ladies immured themselves in her bedchamber in accordance with royal custom. No man was permitted inside, and all functions were taken up by her women. Following directions set down by the king's venerable grandmother, Margaret Beaufort, the room was

> hanged with rich Cloth of Arras [tapestries], sides, roof, windows and all, except one window, which must be hanged so as she [the expectant mother] may have light when it pleaseth her. Then there must be a royal bed, and the floor laid all over and over with carpets, and a cupboard covered with the same suite that the chamber is hanged withal.

The Countess of Richmond was also specific about how the royal bed itself was to be decorated. It should be covered with the finest fabrics, and the canopy above had to be 'of crimson satin embroidered with crowns of gold, the king and queen's arms, and other devices' (in this case the white falcon for Anne). In addition, a pallet bed was required for the actual delivery.

For the next two weeks, there was little for Anne to do but wait. A good deal of her time was spent sitting up in bed directing her cloistered, entirely female court-in-miniature. She appointed her most favorite ladies to keep her company, and their days were devoted to watching over their mistress and entertaining her as best they could in the confines of her bedroom. Even in private with only her women around her, Anne was still expected to look like a queen. Following another directive from the king's grandmother, she was dressed in a nightgown of damask made of crimson cloth-of-gold, and if it got chilly, she had 'a round mantel of crimson velute plain, furred throughout with ermine' to put on. But in the stifling heat of the waning days of summer with nothing but a singular window to let in fresh air, such a garment was seldom needed. This suffocating

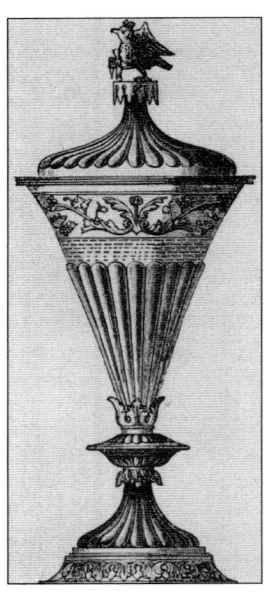

74. Illustration of *The Boleyn Cup* from The Church of St. John the Baptist, Cirencester. (*By an Unknown Artist*)

environment must have been disagreeable to Anne, but the excitement of the impending birth must have compensated for any discomfort she felt.

On 7 September, the momentous day came at last; the culmination of the king's *Great Matter* and his break from Rome. That afternoon, between 3 and 4 o'clock, the child who was to bring forth a new 'golden world' to the English people was born. But to Henry and Anne's shock, it was not a boy, but a 'fair lady'.

Chapter 12

The birth of the new princess was met with rejoicing – but from Anne's enemies. Ambassador Chapuys could not contain his glee when he told the emperor how 'God has entirely abandoned this king, and left him a prey to his own misfortune and to his obstinate blindness, that he may be punished and completely ruined'. The royal couple, Chapuys continued, were extremely upset at the outcome of the childbirth, and the planned celebrations were all cancelled.

Still, Henry and Anne had to put on a good face. Letters were sent out by the king ordering his subjects 'to rejoice and return thanks to the Almighty for having given him an heiress'. Meanwhile, arrangements were made for the child's christening at the Church of the Observant Friars by the palace on 10 September. The godparents were chosen (they being the Archbishop of Canterbury, the Dowager Duchess of Norfolk, and the Dowager Marchioness of Dorset) as was the child's name. She was to be called 'Mary' to the outrage of the supporters of the old queen and her daughter.

Despite her sex, the baby was given a lavish baptism as princess and heiress presumptive. The walls of the church were adorned with rich hangings and the floors covered with sweet-smelling herbs. In the centre was a silver font placed above a platform three steps high so all could see. Among the attendants – some 500 persons in total – were the queen's

75. The Boleyn Cup. (*By Hans Holbein*)

family (the Earl of Wiltshire helping to bear his granddaughter's long train and Viscount Rochford as one of the lords holding up a canopy above his niece), the nobility and the clergy, as well as the Lord Mayor and the civic officials. After the infant was duly christened and confirmed by the Bishop of London, gifts given to her, and refreshments served, she was brought back to the palace to the queen's chamber where she received the blessing of her parents.

The ceremony had gone off superbly, though Chapuys, in his ongoing hatred of Anne Boleyn, described it as 'dull and disagreeable', never mind that he wasn't even present. It was a disheartening affair from the ambassador's point of view, but at least the child was not named 'Mary' like her half-sister after all, but 'Elizabeth' after the king's late mother and Anne's. Chapuys was also glad that the baby was denied the rich christening cloth belonging to the former queen. Anne had demanded it for the ceremony, but Katherine absolutely refused to let her have it. Unlike the jewels Henry VIII had given her which she was forced to concede to her detested rival, the cloth was her personal property which she herself had brought over from Spain. In the end, Anne had to find herself another. Furthermore, there had been no celebratory bonfires or public rejoicing afterwards as the hearts of the people were still with Queen Katherine and Princess Mary.

But to Chapuys' disappointment, the birth of a girl ultimately did not diminish the king's love for 'the concubine', as the envoy continued to denigrate Anne as. According to one of her maids, she had overheard Henry VIII declaring how he would sooner beg door-to-door like a common vagrant than forsake his wife 'whom he loved more than ever'. Nothing further was said of the lady with whom he had had a fling with during the queen's pregnancy, and sure enough, after Anne had recovered from her ordeal and was properly 'churched' (that is she remained in seclusion for about a month to be ritually purified in accordance with religious custom), the royal couple resumed their lovemaking. In the middle of October, it was noticed how 'the king and queen [were] merry'. Henry was confident, as he was in 1516 when Princess Mary was born, that 'by the grace of God, the sons will follow'. Anne would bear him a son next time. Elizabeth's delivery was without complications and proved that her mother was capable of bearing healthy children. The baby was said to be 'beautiful in perfection; in face and proportion' with her colouring taking after her father rather than her mother. Elizabeth had inherited Henry's pale skin and reddish hair instead of Anne's dark looks, though in later life, she would much resemble the latter in face.

* * *

There had not been such a joyous Christmas in years. While the customary holy rites were observed with 'great solemnity' beginning on the eve of Twelvetide on 24 December, the celebratory nature of the season was not forgotten. The palace walls were decorated with festive greenery, under which the Lord of Misrule, or Master of Merry Disports as he was also called, took charge of the 'fine and subtle disguisings, masques, and mummeries'. It was noted that when the former queen was banished in 1531, that Christmas season had been a dismal one as she had taken her women with her, but now with the king's remarriage, the court was brought to life again with Queen Anne and her flock of fun-loving young ladies.

On the Octave Day of Christmas, or rather New Year's Day 1534, a beaming Henry VIII received his courtiers in his Presence Chamber at Greenwich. He was in high spirits as he looked over the crowd gathered in his throne room for the annual tradition of gift giving. It was an opportunity for his courtiers to show their love and loyalty to him by the means of presents, and to be acknowledged by receiving some token in return. Each guest was welcomed as if he or she was the most cherished person in the world to Henry. The king was notorious for his bad temper, but when he chose to be gracious, no man was better at it than he. An Italian, who met Henry in 1531, thought he was 'beyond measure affable', and that he had never met a prince 'better disposed than this one'.

At Henry's side was Queen Anne, her dark eyes taking in the succession of gifts placed in her husband's hands: a book bound in gold into which a clock was inserted, a painting of the hero Hercules, a depiction of Christ, a silver compass covered in gold, a selection of fine jewels, and most popular – purses filled with coins. There was even a monkey to add to the royal menagerie of pets. As impressive and costly as some of the presents were, none, Anne thought proudly, surpassed what she had given the king. Set up for all to see was a magnificent tabletop fountain designed by Hans Holbein, adorned with diamonds, rubies, and pearls. Upon the

76. Design for a Table Fountain. (*By Hans Holbein*)

basin were three golden nymphs whose breasts spouted continuous jets of water to the amusement of all.

After the clergy, the nobles, and the officials presented their gifts and received one in return from Henry VIII – an assortment of plate emblazoned with the royal arms, its value determined by the rank of the recipient – came the queen's women's turn. Their presents to the king were modest, usually articles of clothing or accessories of their own handiwork – shirts, sleeves, garters, handkerchiefs, dog collars, and the like – decorated with exquisite needlework. In thanks, they too received pieces of tableware. Among the ladies were Mistress Marshall, put in charge of Anne's servants; Anne Gainsford, a lady said to be close to the queen; Madge Shelton, a Boleyn cousin; Bess Holland, formerly a laundress to the Duke and Duchess of Norfolk; and Anne Cobham, who was the attendant horsewoman at Anne's coronation. Included in this list was Lady Jane Seymour, a former servant of Katherine of Aragon and perhaps the most recent addition to Anne's staff. It was listed that she gave the king 'a shirt of cambric with a high collar' and was rewarded with 'a gilt cruse with a cover'. However, her new mistress was even more generous. Anne gave Jane and her companions gifts of palfreys and saddles.

The new year brought new hope, and in April, Queen Anne was seen with 'a goodly belly' once again. It was probably in celebration of the good news that a special medal was prepared in her honour, of which a lead prototype still exists, though unfortunately with some later damage to it. The medal depicted Anne as the undoubted Queen of England (by her cipher *A R*, that is *Anna Regina*, and her motto *The Most Happy*). She is shown in bust form, looking very assertive and wearing an English-style gable hood. Around her neck is a large cross denoting Anne as a good Christian ruler. As one historian stated, the medal was undoubtedly produced upon

77. Woodcut of Anne Boleyn's 1534 Medal. (*From Edward Hawkins'* Medallic Illustrations, *1885*)

royal authority, and in that regard, Anne must have taken especial care towards this specimen of her public image.

In addition to the royal medal, Anne was also acknowledged in *The Black Book of the Garter* made in 1534. Created by Lucas Horenbout whom Thomas Boleyn may have helped bring over to England, and who was now employed at court as 'the King's Painter', the illuminated manuscript consisted of the history, ceremonies, and protocols of the 'Most Noble Order of the Garter' founded by King Edward III in the fourteenth century. Within its pages, Henry VIII appears as the present sovereign overseeing the knightly institution, and interestingly, as a stand-in for two of his predecessors, Edward IV and Henry V. Anne, shown crowned and sceptred, and dressed in gold as she holds court, assumes a role in the book too, serving as a model for the first Lady of the Garter, Queen Philippa of Hainault, wife of Edward III. Around Anne's neck is a pendant with her personal cipher *A R* (*Anna Regina*). It was perhaps around this time that she was also honoured by having her heraldic devices and her initial with that of the king's – joined in love knots – carved into the choir screen in King's College Chapel, Cambridge.

Sadly, such tributes proved premature. The prayers to God 'to send us a prince' went unheard as Anne apparently suffered a miscarriage. Chapuys, on the other hand, thought she had never been pregnant at all: she had either false symptoms or she had lied from the start. The latter claim is suspect as it would have been near impossible for Anne to pull off such a deception. Henry VIII had been well informed of her condition as it progressed, and he even had George Boleyn, acting as ambassador to France, tell King Francis that their upcoming second meeting with him had to be postponed till April of the following year, that his wife was 'so far gone with child, she could not cross the sea' with him to Calais. To spare the royal couple embarrassment, it was entirely hushed up as if Anne had never even been pregnant at all. The most poignant reminder of the tragedy was a cradle commissioned from the royal goldsmith Cornelius Hayes. Made of silver and embellished with gemstones, and containing cushions and rich fabrics edged in gold for the child's comfort, it had cost the king the sum of £18 (close to £8,000 today). The cradle was quietly put away and nothing more was said of it.

The miscarriage was a great blow to Anne. Not only had she lost her child, but it undermined her position as queen. She had failed as Katherine

78. The Lady of the Garter. (*By Lucas Horenbout in* The Black Book of the Garter, *1534*)

of Aragon had in the past, and it planted doubt in the king's mind as to whether she was fit to be queen. In September, Henry renewed his attentions to the 'very handsome young lady of this court' with whom he had a flirtation with a year ago. Just as before, Anne did not take it well.

She rounded on Henry only to be slapped down. She ought to be satisfied with what he had done for her, he told Anne roughly. Were he to commence again, he would certainly not do as much!

The new tension at court was exacerbated by the conduct of the queen's sister. That autumn while Anne was quarrelling with the king, Mistress Carey was found to be pregnant. Ever since her husband William's death six years ago, she had been very unhappy: 'all the world did set so little by me', as Mary told Thomas Cromwell. As a widow, she bore the sole responsibility of her two children, and while it would be reasonable to assume that she would quickly remarry – for security if not for love – she did not. Perhaps her former liaisons with Henry VIII and Francis I had tainted her reputation. If so, one William Stafford was willing to overlook Mary's past. As she confessed to Cromwell, even though her lover was younger than she and not of great means, 'love overcame reason … for well I might have had a greater man of birth and a higher, but I ensure you I could never have had one that should have loved me so well, nor a more honest man'.

79. Unknown Lady, Perhaps Mary Boleyn. (*Attributed to Lucas Horenbout*)

But rather than sharing Mary's newfound happiness, the king, the queen, and the Boleyns were scandalized by her secret marriage and the result of it. Even Chapuys, who had no love for Anne and her family, sympathized with them saying that Mary was guilty of 'gross misconduct' and that it would not have been 'honourable or decent for her to appear at court *enceinte*'. Along with her sister's misbehaviour, Anne was particularly offended by a comment of Mary's, one which she undoubtedly took personally. As the now Mistress Stafford declared, she would rather beg her bread with her husband 'than to be the greatest queen in Christendom'. The scandal caused a rift between the two sisters which may have never healed.

* * *

Still without a son on her lap, Anne's subjects remained hostile to her. Whereas a Prince of Wales might have softened their hearts and minds towards the new queen, the birth of a mere girl did not endear them to her. As they did at her coronation where few doffed their caps and many laughed and sneered at her initial combined with the king's – *H A* (read as a mocking Ha! Ha!), the people continued to malign Anne. Among those arrested through Cromwell's network of informants was a Londoner who slandered her as a 'churl's daughter', a woman who called her a 'naughty whore', and another who dared to insult her as a 'goggle-eyed whore' (in reference to Anne's striking eyes?). Not only that, 'God save Queen Katherine!' one of the offenders also said, 'for she was [the] righteous queen, and she trusted to see her queen again!'

Such talk was deemed treasonous by the Act of Succession passed in March 1534. By law, Anne was the sole queen and the king's first marriage 'utterly void and annulled'. Furthermore, until he had a son,

> the said imperial crown … shall be to the issue female between Your Majesty and your said most dear and entirely beloved wife, Queen Anne, begotten, that is to say: first to the eldest issue female, which is the Lady Elizabeth, now princess.

Anyone who denied the king's marriage and his new offspring 'shall be taken and adjudged for misprision of treason'.

But the Act did not deter individuals from speaking their minds. Besides commoners with loose tongues, there were also those of high profile, and thus more dangerous to the crown. Elizabeth Barton for one, who had raved against the king from the start of the *Great Matter* until she was finally hanged that April, had much to say. An angel, the nun claimed, had shown her a series of prophecies. Should the king, 'that infidel Prince of England' refuse to take back Queen Katherine and suppress all heresies, 'the vengeance of God should plague him'. One Elizabeth Amadas also attracted a following. Like the Nun of Kent, she professed supernatural knowledge of things to come. Henry VIII, she forewarned, was the beast of old, the Mouldwarp 'cursed with God's own mouth', who would be the ruin of England and the last of kings. After he was driven from the realm, the mysterious 'Dead Man' – whose coming was heralded by the comet of 1533 – would restore peace

80. Princess Mary. (*By Wenceslaus Hollar after Hans Holbein*)

and order. Even Queen Anne would have her reckoning, warned Mistress Amadas. Already, it had been foretold how 'about this time, this kingdom will be destroyed by a woman', and how a queen would suffer a shameful death according to the divinations of the legendary Merlin. The king's second wife was surely the fulfillment of such prophecies, many believed. The white washing of the White Tower at her crowning signified her doom, cried Mistress Amadas, for she 'should be burned, for she is a harlot'.

There was also opposition to Anne closer to home. For years, the king's daughter Mary had been steadfastly devoted to her mother and jealous of her own position as Princess of England. Shortly after the birth of her half-sister Elizabeth, Mary had been ordered to surrender her title and call herself 'Lady Mary' instead. As an obedient child, she wrote her father, she would defer to him in all things, but she could not 'renounce the titles, rights, and privileges which God, Nature, and her own parents had given her'. Such an answer infuriated Anne. By refusing to acknowledge Elizabeth as the rightful princess and successor of the king, Mary was in fact denying Anne's own queenship. Katherine, isolated and receiving little help from the emperor and the pope, was no threat to Anne, but Mary, young and much loved as her mother was, represented the future – one that might be a threat to Elizabeth. Until Henry VIII had a son, many still considered Mary as his first heir. She was older than her sister, and even though her parents' union had been invalidated, an opinion was that Mary had nevertheless been born in 'good faith' as Henry and Katherine's marriage was fully recognized at the time of her birth.

Initially, Anne thought best to disarm Mary through kindness. If she only recognized her as queen, she told her stepdaughter, she would be better treated than as of late and more importantly, be reconciled to her father.

But far from being receptive, the teenager was defiant, even insulting. She knew of no other queen, Mary said, than her mother Katherine, but if the *king's mistress* could do her the kindness of speaking to the king on her behalf, she would be most grateful. Anne was incensed and after further rebuffs from Mary, she finally gave up, vowing to put down her 'proud Spanish blood'. Anne was also heard to say that should the king ever leave the realm and put her in charge as regent, she would see to it that Mary was executed as a traitor.

81. Philippe Chabot, Admiral De Brion. (*By an Unknown Artist*)

Even when Lord Rochford warned her against doing such an audacious thing, Anne boasted she would not be afraid to strike, 'even if she were to be burnt or flayed alive in consequence'. 'The princess will be the cause of my death unless I get rid of her beforehand, but I will so manage that if I die before her, she shall not laugh at me,' Anne promised.

No matter how much she threatened Mary, Anne was actually powerless to do anything against her. The king, despite his anger at her obstinacy, still had a soft spot for his daughter, and Mary's own international standing served to protect her from harm. The continuing esteem for the princess was made clear to Anne in November 1534. When Philippe Chabot, Admiral De Brion and the ambassador of France, arrived at court, he was seen to be overly friendly to his counterpart Eustace Chapuys and oddly cold towards Anne herself. Also, the French envoy spoke at great length about Mary, calling her 'the most singular and valuable gem in all this kingdom'.

The reason for Chabot's lavish praise was made obvious when he later met with Henry VIII. Instead of a marriage alliance between the King of France's third son Charles, Duke of Angoulême, and the Princess Elizabeth, Chabot said his master wanted Mary instead. Henry and

Anne were flabbergasted. The proposal was thought to be a 'hoax or mere joke on the part of the admiral' at first, but Chabot was entirely serious. Only after much renegotiation was King Francis, whom Anne had always thought of as her friend and ally, willing to accept her daughter instead. But as the months went by, it was evident that the French were dragging their heels. In February 1535, when the representative Palamedes Gontier came for further talks, Anne spoke to him in private. He must hasten the alliance, she begged him, 'so that she may not be ruined and lost, for she sees herself very near that, and in more grief and trouble than before her marriage'. She was in such a state of fear that 'she could not write, nor see him again, nor stay longer' as she thought herself being spied on, even by the king. As soon as she heard Henry coming, Anne quickly left the room, leaving Gontier speechless.

Part IV

Ira principis mors est.
　　　　　　　(The wrath of the prince is death)

Chapter 13

In the summer of 1535, a great progress was planned that would take the royal couple and their court-on-the-move from Windsor Castle to Oxfordshire, then to Gloucestershire, and then down to Wiltshire and Hampshire before finally returning in the autumn. Anne was no doubt excited and relieved at this long holiday in store for them both. Lately, the king was reportedly ignoring his wife and 'more occupied with dancing parties and ladies than ever he was'.

Apart from Henry's philandering, Anne had also been on edge with the unceasing hatred directed towards her. The people continued to blame her for the displacement of Queen Katherine and Princess

82. John Fisher, Bishop of Rochester. (*By Philip Galle*)

Mary, and things worsened when many were put to death for their sake. In May, eighteen Carthusian monks belonging to the London Charterhouse were dragged upon hurdles to the place of execution at Tyburn. There, each one was hanged and quickly cut down before he was dead, only to then be butchered alive as the crowd watched in revulsion. Their heads and their dismembered parts were subsequently distributed throughout the city – even to the Charterhouse itself – as a warning to others who denied the king his title of Supreme Head of the Church. In June, Bishop Fisher went to his death as well. Unlike the monks, Henry VIII spared the old man the agony of being hanged and quartered. He merely died by the axe, as did Thomas More, the former Lord Chancellor, a fortnight later. The king was widely condemned for putting such respected men to death, and according to Chapuys, Henry was so perverse that just two days after Fisher was dead, he attended an anti-clerical play in which the heads of priests were lopped off. He enjoyed it so much that he sent a message to his wife that she ought to catch a performance herself.

By the time the summer progress was underway in early July, Anne was in a better frame of mind. She gave no thought anymore to the events

83. Acton Court in the 19th Century. (*By P. Oushton*)

of late, but only to the future ahead of her. Leaving behind all worries, she and Henry could renew their love. It would be a like second honeymoon for them – Calais being their first where they may have begun to sleep together. Together, with only a select company of their favourites, they would travel and see the west at their leisure as far as Bristol, and with the 'grease season' approaching, there would also be the thrill of the chase to be enjoyed. As the weeks passed, the couple were described as being very 'merry' together, just as Anne had hoped they would be.

84. Sir Nicholas Poyntz. (*By Hans Holbein*)

As the progress was set to last until October, accommodations for the royal party had to be made well in advance. Royal properties along the way would be put to use, and where there were none, Henry and Anne were welcomed into the homes of the well-to-do gentry who had been warned to be ready to receive them. Near the village of Iron Acton in Gloucestershire, Nicholas Poyntz went so far as to quickly add a whole new section to his ancestral home Acton Court – 'a goodly house and two parks by the house, one of red deer, another of fallow' – just for Henry and Anne for their two days stay in August. The Poyntz family had been in favour with the Tudors since the reign of Henry VII, and Nicholas himself was a familiar face to the king and queen having accompanied them to Calais three years ago. He was also keen on religious reform, as were a good many of the others hosting Henry and Anne that summer. Thus, the progress was not entirely all pleasure, as it was the king's intention at the same time to consolidate support in the west for his new policies. But even those who remained conservative in their beliefs but were nonetheless loyal to the crown, were also honoured with a royal visit. In early September, Henry and Anne stopped at Wolfhall, the family home of her lady-in-waiting Jane Seymour. Whether Jane had joined the progress is unknown, but the couple were entertained by her father Sir John who had long done service to the Tudors. That the Seymours were in good favour was evident when

142   Anne Boleyn

the king and his suite then graced the home of Jane's brother Edward in Elvetham before they made their way back to Windsor in October.

* * *

The French ambassador, who met the king and queen on their summer progress, gave them the regards of Margaret of Angoulême. Anne was equally cordial and she returned a message that her 'greatest wish, next to having a son, is to see you again'. Anne's former attachment to Margaret had made a great impact upon her religious views. According to Roger Twysden, Anne 'first learned the grounds of Protestant religion' from King Francis's sister. While Margaret (and Anne for that matter) was never actually a Protestant, she was a committed reformist, so much so that when the French Calvinist, Théodore Beza, compiled a collection of

85. Margaret of Angoulême. (*From Theodore Beza's* Les vrais pourtraits des hommes illustrés, *1581*)

biographies of notables engaged in the new faith, Margaret was included – the only woman to be fully honoured that way.

Anne herself would later be given much credit for the English Reformation. According to the martyrologist John Foxe, 'during her life, the religion of Christ most happily flourished and had a right prosperous course', and John Aylmer, Bishop of London, even paid tribute to Anne as 'the chief, first, and only cause of the banishing the beast of Rome with all his beggarly baggage'. Even though the extent of Anne's influence remains controversial, there is no doubt as to her commitment to religious reform.

Concerning the practice of her faith, Anne, like her brother with whom she was very close and who believed as she did, was especially devoted to the reading of Scripture. Anne owned a French Bible translated by the humanist Jacques Lefevre d'Etaples who received the patronage of Margaret of Angoulême. She also had two other works of his: *Epistres et evangiles des cinquante et deux semaines de l'an* and *L'Ecclesiaste* (by the German Protestant reformer Johannes Brenz that d'Etaples made a translation of) which she had her 'most loving and friendly brother' render into English. While Anne did show interest in some radical works as well,

86. Nicholas Bourbon. (*By Francesco Bartolozzi after Hans Holbein*)

they were largely of an anti-papal nature which Henry VIII himself gave his stamp of approval (like the works of Simon Fish and William Tyndale mentioned before), and nothing so extreme as to get her accused of heresy.

Anne worked actively towards reform, both before and after her marriage. Apart from introducing the king to newfangled books, she had lent her help to those persecuted for their faith. When the cleric Thomas Forman was arrested by Cardinal Wolsey for possessing Lutheran writings, Anne stepped in and secured his release. She did likewise for one Thomas Alwaye who had also fallen foul of the cardinal. Later as queen, Anne continued to look after those in need, even from abroad. When a woman named Mistress Marye left France for safer shores in England 'for religion's sake', Anne received her and put her under her protection. She also welcomed the French scholar and poet Nicholas Bourbon. Bourbon, who had also been acquainted with Margaret of Angoulême, had been imprisoned in his native country for his outspoken anti-papalism. Hearing of Anne's magnanimity, he asked for her help through Doctor William Butts. Anne was able to persuade Henry VIII to get Bourbon released and to even bring him over to England. He was maintained at the queen's expense and was appointed as a tutor to her nephew Henry Carey and other youths at court. Were it not for Anne's intercession, a grateful Bourbon later wrote, he would still be in prison, 'chained in that darkness, unhappily languishing, still under restraint'.

Butts, who had acted as Bourbon's intermediary, was also instrumental in bringing other evangelicals to the queen's attention. The royal doctor was inclined to reform himself and had been educated at Cambridge University where he befriended many co-religionists. Through this network, Anne, who 'favoured good letters and learning,' recruited men such as Hugh Latimer, Nicholas Shaxton, William Betts, William Latymer, and John Skip to her service as clergymen. She also supported scholars financially, giving one individual a yearly sum of £40 (about £17,700 today) to complete his studies outside the country. Furthermore, Anne was responsible for relieving Cambridge and Oxford from 'tenths and subsidies', a form of taxation.

Anne was determined to encourage piety at court as well. While the merry 'pastime' following her coronation undoubtedly still went on in her apartments, Anne did try to instil a new morality among her staff. Her ladies were told to conduct themselves with 'modesty and chastity',

87. Title Page of The English Bible with *HA* cipher, 1535.

and to edify themselves through religious readings. Anne set herself as an example by 'exercising herself continually in reading the French Bible and other French books of like effect'. The former was her copy of *La Saincte Bible en Francoys* of 1534, translated by Jacques Lefevre d'Etaples. It was beautifully bound and stamped in gold, emphasizing its importance to Anne, and upon the cover was a crowned Tudor rose between the royal initials *HA*. As for her servants, a large English Bible (translated by William Tyndale) was set up upon a lectern so that 'every person might have recourse to read upon [it] when they would'.

88. William Tyndale. (*By François van Bleyswijck*)

Anne's commitment to reform also had her being distrustful of ignorant practices of worship. During a visit to Syon Abbey in Middlesex, she found the Bridgettine nuns prostrate on the ground praying in Latin together. Anne admonished them for uttering words few of them understood, and she offered the sisters prayer books in English to use instead. Anne also dedicated herself to rooting out idolatry. During her summer progress with the king, they had passed through Gloucestershire, and Anne was intrigued by the famed Holy Blood of Hailes. Obtained in the thirteenth century, the blood was believed to be that of Christ Himself shed on the cross, and it was placed in a crystal container for veneration. The so-called blood remained fresh for centuries and attracted countless pilgrims who left offerings, making the Abbey of Hailes very wealthy. Perhaps Anne had learnt about it from Hugh Latimer, whom she had appointed one of her chaplains. In 1533, he had made a complaint to the authorities about the relic as a focus of superstition. As a result, Anne launched an investigation into it and it was later determined to be 'but the blood of some duck or as some say, red wax'. For her many efforts, Anne was acknowledged as 'the first princess that might justly vaunt the restitution of the truth and the overthrow of the pestiferous crept into the Church of Christ'.

Chapter 14

On 9 January 1536, a great ball was held at Greenwich. For the occasion, Anne dressed herself in festive yellow, and except for a white feather to his cap, Henry too was in the same golden colour from head to foot. The couple's gaudy apparel was in response to the good news of late. Two days earlier, Katherine of Aragon had died at Kimbolton Castle in Cambridgeshire. Abandoned and not allowed to see her daughter for years, the unhappy queen passed away in the presence of her friend Maria de Salinas, who had come to England with her from Spain so very long ago. Maria had shared Katherine's trials and tribulations, and at the end, fulfilled her mistress's last wish not to die 'alone like a beast'. Even in her last hours, Katherine refused to speak ill of the king, and in that regard, maintained that not even death could take away her title of Queen of England.

Far from mourning his ex-wife, Henry VIII was elated. His 'joy and delight' was entirely repugnant to Chapuys. The envoy, who had visited Katherine shortly before she died and thought that she looked reasonably well in spite of her illness, harboured suspicions that she had been done away with by poison. But as much as Anne had wished her dead over the years, Katherine's death appeared to have been entirely natural. Her demise was welcome tidings, so much so that Anne rewarded the messenger with a rich gift and 'made great demonstration of joy' as the king did. Their daughter, the princess Elizabeth, was brought out and taken to church 'to the sound of trumpets and with great display', and Anne watched proudly as Henry – a most doting father when he chose to be – then carried the little girl about, showing her off to his courtiers. The celebrations over Katherine's death went on for days, and in his jubilation, Henry spent hours at the tiltyard in mock combat as the champion of his lady, the queen and the mother of his son-to-be. Anne, to his delight, was pregnant again.

89. King Solomon and the Queen of Sheba. (*By Wenceslaus Hollar after Hans Holbein*). Solomon is probably a likeness of Henry VIII, while the Queen of Sheba may be a representation of Anne Boleyn.

As the child grew in her womb, Anne fortified herself in the belief that despite her miscarriage in the year before, come summer she would indeed give the king his male heir. But her hopes were thwarted by tragedy once again. On 24 January, Henry rode in a joust and as he clashed lances with his challenger, he was knocked to the ground. Both rider and horse fell so heavily 'that everyone thought it a miracle he was not killed'. The news was conveyed to the queen by the Duke of Norfolk – a tactless and insensitive man – in such an abrupt manner that his niece 'took a fright'. While Henry did recover from his fall, Anne, in her distress, miscarried of a boy five days later. While she lay in sorrow, it did not go unnoticed that Katherine of Aragon was laid to rest at Peterborough Abbey that very same day. To Anne's enemies, the death of her child was retribution for her treatment of the old queen. Needless to say, Chapuys felt no pity for her either. He even accused Anne of unfairly blaming Norfolk for her mishap, and as for Henry, his accident was a prelude to a 'greater misfortune' in store for him.

* * *

The death of Katherine of Aragon ironically brought about a rapprochement between England and the Holy Roman Empire. Charles V, despite his commiseration for his aunt, had been too practical a politician to engage in open conflict for the sake of their family honour. Now with her gone and knowing that England's amity with France was beginning to fray, Charles instructed Chapuys to make overtures of friendship on his behalf. His mission, it can be imagined, was unpleasant to the envoy. He continued to believe that Queen Katherine had succumbed to poison, and it was his great regret that when she was still alive, she had always refused to condone a rebellion against Henry VIII as he had advised. Besides being an act of treason, Katherine, who continued to maintain that she was the king's true wife, adamantly would not take up arms against her own husband.

Nevertheless, the emperor had to be obeyed, and Chapuys promised to do his best to win over the English king. But before his audience with Henry, Chapuys spoke to Thomas Cromwell first. The two had got along well, and Chapuys was glad to know that he was most eager for a renewed Anglo-Imperial alliance. At their meeting, Chapuys could not help but notice, he told the emperor, how high Cromwell had risen lately in his master's favour. Their talk had taken place at his new 'very fine house', which Henry VIII had gifted him and which was completely furnished to boot.

When Chapuys arrived at court on the morning of 18 April, he was given a warm welcome by members of the King's Council. It was 'such a cordial and honourable reception that nothing better could be wished for,' the ambassador thought. Even Lord Rochford was most courteous, signalling the Boleyns' desire for the emperor's friendship as well. On

90. The Entry of Charles V and Pope Clement VII into Bologna. (*By Nicolaas Hogenberg*)

his part, Chapuys commended George for his desire for peace, but he purposely avoided any mention of religion as the young man would surely give him a mouthful of his 'Lutheran principles, of which he is so proud that he cannot abstain from boasting of them in public'. Anne's own willingness to win the Hapsburgs' goodwill was made clear at an incident later that day. When Chapuys attended Mass with the rest of the court, he was placed by the door within Anne's sight as she entered the chapel. When she passed, Chapuys in politeness made a bow with the rest. As all eyes turned towards the queen for her reaction, she stopped and turned around. Instead of snubbing him for his past hostility towards her, she graciously returned his greeting with a curtsy of her own.

With the Council and even the hated Anne being so accommodating – she was even heard to badmouth her old ally the French at dinner – Chapuys expected an easy negotiation with Henry VIII. It was anything but. When the emperor insisted that his cousin Mary be restored as princess and that the king should make up with the papacy, Henry was furious. How he treated his daughter was his own affair, he fumed, 'nobody had anything to do with that', and as for his dealings with the Vatican, that too did not concern Charles either. He especially resented, he then shouted, how his own nephew was treating him as if he were a child telling him what to do. Henry then listed the various wrongs – true or not – that the emperor had inflicted upon him, and how unappreciative he had always been, Why, if not for his help, Henry went on in a tirade, Charles would never had been made emperor in the first place, and he was also an ingrate for working against him in the matter of his divorce. From what he had been told, Henry said, Charles had even gone so far as to pressure the pope to deprive him of his throne. As Chapuys defended his master from this onslaught of accusations, he noticed how Cromwell became more and more agitated at the king's behaviour. At one point, he became so exasperated that he had to excuse himself and call for a drink.

Henry VIII's refusal to make up with the emperor showed that he was still firmly committed to his marriage – at least for the time being. Still, Anne's recent miscarriage had significantly weakened her hold over him, and his eyes began to wander again. By early February, Henry was paying court to one of the queen's own ladies, Jane Seymour, and he was even giving her presents. When Chapuys heard about this latest development, he made little of Jane. In contrast to her mistress, Mistress Seymour was mousey in appearance and dull in manner, so much so that she could hardly hold Henry's interest for long or so it seemed. Actually, it was Jane's dissimilarity from Anne that had attracted Henry to her and she used this to her advantage. She was unassuming and made no scenes, and from the king's point of view, a welcome distraction from his tempestuous and demanding wife.

91. Jane Seymour. (*By Nicholas Hilliard*)

Interestingly, Jane Seymour's qualities that drew the king to her might well have been the very same that won her a place at court. While her brother Sir Edward Seymour, a rising courtier, might have initiated her placement in the queen's household, it was ultimately Anne's decision as mistress to accept Jane or not. Ever aware of the king's attentions to the lovely ladies of the court, perhaps Anne thought the seemingly harmless Jane to be of no threat to her and allowed her a position. The young woman would make a good servant as she appeared to be docile and obedient. However, Anne underestimated her. Jane, despite her outward conformity to the great changes in the kingdom, did not care for the queen's evangelical views nor did she personally like her. Jane was religiously conservative, and during her past service to Queen Katherine, she was wholly in sympathy with her and her daughter Princess Mary. Jane had not intentionally set out to challenge Anne, but once she had attracted the king's notice, those who were still likewise devoted to Katherine's memory and to the reinstatement of the princess, eagerly recruited Jane to their cause.

As Anne did before her, Jane refused the king her bed unless he offered her a future. Her terms were made obvious to him when he sent her a gift of money in late March. Instead of receiving it, she went on bended knee and asked the messenger to tell Henry that as she valued her honour which she would not forsake 'even if she were to die a thousand deaths', she could not accept his present nor read his letter (presumably a love note). However, Jane said with meaning, she *would* be agreeable when 'God would be pleased to send her some advantageous marriage'. Jane was angling for a wedding ring. Far from putting him off, Henry was even more inflamed with love. He praised Jane for her virtue and he promised not to see her again except with her relatives about as chaperones. In keeping with his promise, Henry had Cromwell ejected from his rooms at court and gave them to Edward Seymour and his wife so that he might visit Jane in their presence for propriety's sake.

92. Sir Edward Seymour. (*By Jacob Houbraken*)

Being 'quite resolved' that she would only be his if he made her queen, Jane, following the advice of Princess Mary's supporters, advised the king how much his subjects hated his marriage 'and that not one considers it legitimate'. Because it was still treason to deny his union with Queen Anne, Jane was playing a dangerous game. If Henry was in a mood and she had brought up the subject in an ill-timed moment, she would surely have been in trouble. But the king, tiring of Anne, was willing to listen, especially as Jane was backed by her friends who conveniently stood by to voice their agreement. Whether or not Anne knew of her intrigues, Henry's attentions to Jane and her willingness to accept them were enough to drive her into a frenzy. She reacted with violence it was said, subjecting her rival to her 'scratching and by-blows'.

Whatever harm Anne might do to her, there was no escaping the fact that Jane and her supporters were gaining the upper hand. No longer did the queen's father and brother have the king's ear only, but also men like Edward Seymour, Nicholas Carew, and Francis Bryan (a Boleyn cousin no less) who sensing which the way the wind was blowing, began to work against the queen. An ominous sign that April for Anne and her family was Lord Rochford's failure to be made a Knight of the Garter. George's admittance would have been another feather to the Boleyns' cap. His father Sir Thomas, being 'every way worthy of this most renowned order,' had achieved that very honour in 1523. However, the knighthood went to Carew instead, as 'the largest number of votes fell upon him, [and] as because he was to be deemed highly fitting by reason of the glory of his family and reputation'.

Even more troubling for Anne and her party was the desertion of Thomas Cromwell. Although he and the queen shared the same religious sympathies – Martin Luther would soon praise Cromwell for his 'goodwill in the cause of Christ' – politically they had grown apart. When the Church of England yielded its authority to the king, a thorough assessment of its riches was made under the direction of Cromwell in his new position of Vice-Gerent in Spirituals. Armed with this evaluation of the Church's wealth, an anti-clerical Parliament decreed that religious houses with an income of less that £200 (about £86,000 today) per year were to be dissolved and their assets surrendered to the crown. It was Anne's intention that this money should go towards educational and charitable purposes, but Cromwell had it funnelled into the king's pockets instead.

93. Sir Nicholas Carew. (*By Hans Holbein*)

In this standoff of queen versus minister, Anne had made her displeasure known at a sermon preached on Passion Sunday. Her almoner John Skip told the congregation the story of good Queen Esther, the wife of the Persian ruler Ahasuerus. The king's vizier, the wicked Haman, had plotted the destruction of the Jews, but Esther went before her husband and pleading with him, moved him to mercy. To the congregants, Skip's meaning was clear. Queen Anne, another Esther, was begging Henry VIII (King Ahasuerus) to spare the religious houses from pillaging by Cromwell (Haman).

94. Procession of the Knights of the Garter (by Joseph Sympson after Lucas Horenbout in *The Black Book of the Garter*, 1534. From left to right are: Charles Brandon (Duke of Suffolk), Henry Courtney (Marquess of Exeter), William Fitzalan (Earl of Arundel), George Talbot (Earl of Shrewsbury), Henry Percy (Earl of Northumberland), Henry Bourchier (Earl of Essex), Arthur Plantagenet (Lord Lisle), Ralph Neville (Earl of Westmorland), George Neville, (Lord Abergavenny), Robert Radcliffe (Earl of Sussex), Walter Devereux (Lord Ferrers), Thomas Manners (Earl of Rutland), Thomas Darcy (Lord Darcy), Anne de Montmorency (Grand Master of France), Thomas Boleyn (Earl of Wiltshire), and John de Vere (Earl of Oxford).

95. Queen Esther Before King Ahasuerus. (*By Lucas van Leyden*)

Skip's sermon caused a sensation at court, but Cromwell himself was not ignorant of the queen's antipathy for him. As he had told Chapuys, during one of his confrontations with Anne, she had raged at him saying how she 'would like to see his head off his shoulders'. It was not an idle threat. In the Biblical account of Queen Esther, Haman was subsequently hanged by King Ahasuerus. Cromwell had never forgotten the destruction of his mentor Cardinal Wolsey, and as he confided to Chapuys,

> he was well aware of the precarious nature of human affairs, to say nothing of those appertaining to royal courts; he had for a long time back known this, having had continually before his eyes several examples of it of a domestic nature. He had, however, admitted to himself that the day might come when fate would strike him as it had struck his predecessors in office: then he would arm himself with patience and place himself for the rest in the hands of God.

For his very survival, Cromwell then decided, he must go on the offensive. It was either him or Anne. She must be taken down, lest he, like Haman, find himself on the gallows.

* * *

In the weeks following her attack on Cromwell, Anne felt some measure of safety. The king had still not given in to the emperor and he remained firmly committed to their marriage. In a letter – dated 25 April – addressed to his ambassador at the Imperial court, Henry VIII continued to complain of Charles's 'ingratitude' and 'unkindness', and he referred to Anne as 'our most dear and most entirely beloved wife the queen.' Furthermore, a trip to Dover was planned for the two of them in early May.

But while her title of queen remained secure by all appearances, Henry continued to see Jane Seymour. Anne could only hope that he would tire of his new mistress and come to love his wife again as he used to. In the meanwhile, Anne found solace in her daughter the princess. Despite her initial disappointment at her sex, Anne became very attached to the pretty and precocious little girl. Unfortunately, protocol demanded that Elizabeth be set up in her own household, and at 3 months old, she had been sent away to Hatfield House in Hertfordshire to be raised by a governess. From a distance, Anne kept up with her daughter's progress, and in October 1534, the infant, 'with the assent of the queen's grace', began her weaning. Anne visited Elizabeth when she was able, and she

96. Hatfield House in the 18th Century. (*By Francesco Sesone*)

looked to it that her daughter was always well provided for in her clothes and other necessities.

Mindful of Elizabeth's spiritual upbringing as well, Anne had a meeting with one of her chaplains, Matthew Parker, around 26 April. Like some other clergymen in her service, Parker had been recruited from Cambridge University, and Anne had been so impatient to have him that John Skip had to write twice to him in one day to tell him to hurry to court. Anne became particularly fond of Parker and because of that, she committed her daughter into his pastoral care when they spoke together. Decades later, Parker would recall his conversation with the queen and the profound impact it had on him in terms of rendering service to Elizabeth.

Anne also found comfort in the company of her friends who remained loyal to her. With such persons, she could be at ease and engage in a more familiar manner than she would with others at court. One of her favourites was Sir Henry Norris who was also close to the king. Norris served in Henry's Privy Chamber and later became his Groom of the Stool (that is his lavatory attendant). The position made Norris the king's most intimate servant and gave him access to his master as no one else had. On 29 April, Anne asked Norris, a widower, why he had

97. Matthew Parker. (*By George Vertue after an Unknown Artist*)

not remarried? He would wait a while, he answered. 'You look for dead men's shoes,' Anne joked, 'for if ought come to the king but good, you would look to have me.' Far from being amused, Norris was astounded that Anne would say such a thing, suggesting that if Henry VIII were dead, he would make her his wife. If he should entertain such a thought, Norris protested, 'he would his head were off'. What began as silly banter on Anne's part erupted into an argument. She was offended that Norris took her so seriously, and she threatened to 'undo him if she would'. To make matters worse, their heated words were overheard.

The king was furious when word got to him of the quarrel between his wife and his servant. Not only had she debased herself in suggesting an intimacy between them, but she had dared to imply his death – an act of high treason. Even when Anne, in an attempt to do damage control, had Norris make a public declaration that she was a 'good woman' who was innocent of any sexual impropriety, Henry remained angry. He was still upset when Anne approached him the next day, with the baby Elizabeth in her arms no less, in an attempt to soothe his rage. Observing them from an open window above, Henry pointedly ignored his wife and daughter, and he returned to a meeting with his Council. By the tension in the air, it was obvious to everyone present, even Anne, 'that some deep and difficult question was being discussed'.

Chapter 15

Henry and Anne were a volatile couple, but all seemed to be well between them again at the May Day tournament at Greenwich. The king had seemingly forgotten the incident between his wife and Norris, and when the latter was in need of a horse for the joust, Henry kindly lent him his. But as Anne cheered on her brother Lord Rochford and his team acting as challengers versus Norris and his band as defenders, a message was brought to the king. After perusing its contents, he suddenly got up and left. He also gave an order for Norris to accompany him.

The king and Norris's sudden departure left the spectators in bewilderment, 'chiefly the queen'. Anne was just as perplexed the next day when the Council asked to see her. A delegation, headed by the Duke of Norfolk and joined by Thomas Cromwell, incredibly accused of high treason. No specifics were given except that three men had been arrested as she herself was now too. Astonished and frightened, Anne was given little time to prepare herself before she was taken to a barge headed for the Tower of London.

During the river journey, Anne proclaimed her innocence, but only Sir William Paulet, the king's comptroller, had a kind word for her. The rest were grim-faced, including Norfolk who berated his niece along the way. At 5 o'clock in the afternoon, the barge arrived at its destination. Three years before, the Tower had been a place of triumph for Anne, now it would serve as her prison. William Kingston who had accompanied Anne from Greenwich, led her – as he had done at her coronation – up the river steps and across Tower Wharf to the drawbridge at the Byward Tower. At her entry, Anne finally lost her composure. She dropped to her knees and began sobbing. In between her tears, she prayed aloud for mercy as she was 'not guilty of her accusement', and she asked the departing king's men to speak well of her to their master.

98. Sir William Paulet. (*By an Unknown Artist*)

With the walls seemingly closing in around her, Anne asked if she was to be held in a dungeon. No, said Kingston – now her gaoler – she was to be put up in the royal palace as she was during her last stay. The relief was too much for Anne, and again, she collapsed into a fit of weeping, but this time followed by bouts of wild laughter, a strange pattern of behaviour Kingston would witness over the course of her imprisonment. When Anne wondered if she would die without a fair hearing, she even laughed when her jailer reassured her that even 'the poorest subject the king hath, hath justice'. Was she doing so in mockery? In the days to follow, Anne would waver between hope and despair. 'One hour she is determined to die, and the next hour much contrary to that,' Kingston reported to Cromwell. That she might be delivered from her ordeal, Anne requested that the Blessed Sacrament be placed in her closet in her chamber so 'that she might pray for mercy'. She also tried to make a direct appeal – not to the king but to Cromwell. When she asked for permission to write him a letter, Kingston declined. He was only permitted to deliver a verbal message on her behalf.

When she was not in terror and sorrow, Anne assumed a brave front as if she had not a care in the world. She would sometimes be 'very merry' calling for a 'great dinner', and then shortly be asking for her supper. Surely, she said, the king was merely testing her and soon she would be set free. All of England was praying for her, Anne reassured herself, especially the clergymen she had raised to prominence. But in truth, none came to her defence. Her almoner John Skip dared not, nor did Matthew Parker. Nicholas Shaxton even went as far as to denounce the queen for her 'misconduct' that slandered the Gospel and for her 'vice' which 'had not the like in Christendom'. Only Thomas Cranmer had the courage to write to the king on her behalf, but only in the most cautious terms:

> I am clean amazed, for I had never better opinion of woman; but I think Your Highness would not have gone so far if she had not been culpable. I was most bound to her of all creatures living, and therefore beg that I may, with Your Grace's favour, wish and pray that she may declare herself innocent.

However, if she was indeed found guilty, the archbishop continued, 'there is not one that loveth God and His Gospel that ever will favour her, but must hate her above all other', including himself. And he was prepared to do that, or so Cranmer said, when evidence was then presented to him affirming the queen's guilt, for which he was sorry.

But what was this proof and what exactly had Anne been charged with? When she herself asked Kingston why she was in the Tower, he was elusive. All she knew at first was that Henry Norris and the young musician Mark Smeaton (who had gone with her and the king to Calais and was a fixture at court) had been apprehended as well. In a moment of despair, Anne had cried out aloud wondering if it was Norris who had accused her and that they would die together? But then her mood – always mercurial – quickly changed, and she told Kingston, 'For I am as clear from the company of man as for sin as I am clear from you, and am the king's true wedded wife.' Anne's allusion to infidelity on her part was indeed part of the charges against her. When Henry VIII confronted Norris on their ride to Westminster after the May Day joust, he demanded to know if he had slept with his wife? He even offered the man a pardon 'in case he would utter the truth'. Norris wholly denied it and found himself in the Tower the next day.

As for Mark Smeaton, he had been examined at Cromwell's house on 30 April – probably under torture or at least the threat of it – and admitted to sexual intercourse with the queen. His confession was almost certainly the mysterious message conveyed to the king at the tournament the next day. All Anne had to say about Smeaton was that she had once found him loitering about her room looking sad. When she asked him what the matter was, he sighed and said it was nothing. Annoyed at what

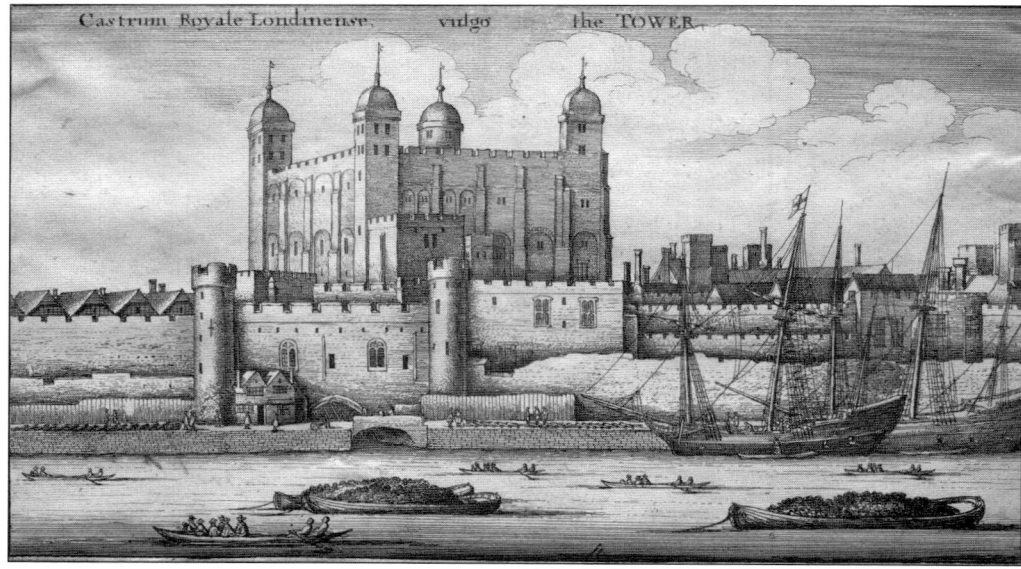

99. The Tower of London. (*By Wenceslaus Hollar*)

she perceived to be posturing on his part to attract her attention, Anne scolded him: 'You may not look to have me speak to you as I should a nobleman because you are an inferior person.' Humbled, Smeaton made a hasty retreat.

In the next couple of days, Anne learnt of more men taken into custody. Her old friend Thomas Wyatt had been charged in conjunction with her, as were two courtiers, William Brereton and Richard Page. The two had served in the king's Privy Chamber, and like Norris and Smeaton, were part of his suite to Calais. But it was Francis Weston who gave Anne cause for fear, even more than Norris as she herself admitted. That April, she had chided Weston for pursuing her cousin Madge Shelton instead of being with his wife. He answered saying he loved another instead. 'Who is that?' Anne asked? 'It is yourself,' Weston replied cheekily. She thought him impudent and 'defied him'. Now, Anne must have realized that his words would certainly be twisted into a charge of adultery between them.

But the most awful news was that of Lord Rochford. At her arrest, Anne was told that her 'sweet brother' was last seen at Whitehall. What Kingston failed to add was that George Boleyn was then taken to the Tower that very same day as she was. It is not clear when Anne was informed of the charge against them both, but it must have come as a shock when she knew of it. Like the other six men, Rochford was accused of having sex with the queen, albeit she was his own sister. The charge was allegedly made by his wife Lady Rochford. Jane Parker was thought to have provided evidence of incest out of jealousy of the close relationship between her husband and Anne, and perhaps to abandon the sinking ship that was the Boleyns. This belief and her subsequent role in the downfall of Henry VIII's later wife Katheryn Howard – she was accused of aiding and abetting the young queen's adultery – had Lady Rochford going down in infamy. However, there is no solid proof that Jane worked against Anne and George. She had nothing to gain if they fell, and when they did, she was reduced to being a 'poor desolate widow' as she lamented to Thomas Cromwell.

But what did Henry VIII himself make of all this? On the very day of his wife's arrest, he wept before his son Henry Fitzroy. He embraced the young man and told him how thankful he and his sister Mary ought to be 'for having escaped from the hands of that woman, who had planned their death by poison'. But Henry's tears were momentary; soon he was carousing on the river making a great show of it. He was seen visiting one house and then another till late into the night, and always with a harem of ladies. His new found happiness was like 'the joy and pleasure a man feels in getting rid of a thin, old, and vicious hack in the hope of getting soon a fine horse to ride,' Chapuys noted cynically. Henry was a humiliated horned cuckold, but he seemed not to mind a bit, the ambassador added. Though the king believed that his wife had had her way with up to a hundred men, 'you never saw a prince or husband show or wear his horns more patiently and lightly than this one does'. In fact, Henry even bragged about having written a tragedy of the whole affair, as he had long suspected the queen.

In truth, while the self-pitying Henry came to blame Anne as an enchantress who had beguiled him into marriage, the suspicions of adultery were not put into play until the queen's fall was engineered – a scheme 'planned and brought about' by Cromwell who was 'authorised and commissioned by the king' to do so, as the minister himself admitted to Chapuys. In readiness, an inquiry (a court of *oyer and terminer*) had been established to hear charges of treason as early as 24 April. As Cromwell also told Chapuys, this was in response to rumours coming from Flanders of a conspiracy to kill the king in which the queen was

100. Westminster from the River. (*By Wenceslaus Hollar*)

involved. If regicide was indeed the original sole charge against Anne and the seven other men, perhaps she herself then unwittingly added fuel to the fire with her flirtatious talk with Henry Norris. Whether Henry VIII truly thought that his wife was an 'accursed whore' who was plotting his death so she could take up with others will always be a mystery, but it appears that he allowed himself to believe the worst of her in order to square his conscience and to justify his callous disposal of her.

On 12 May, the commoners accused with the queen were taken to Westminster Hall – once the scene of Anne's celebratory banquet following her coronation – for their trial. As Norris, Brereton, Weston, and Smeaton (Wyatt and Page were released as the charges were dropped) stood in the vast chamber, now transformed into a court of law, they heard how their alleged crimes had come to light. Sir Anthony Browne, the prosecution said, had been told by his sister Elizabeth, the Countess of Worcester, how her royal mistress was making love to Norris and others, including her own brother Lord Rochford. Horrified by what he learnt, Sir Anthony, upon his allegiance to the king, revealed the queen's offences. The accusation, the jury heard, was corroborated by other ladies close to the queen, including one who was particularly dear to her, a certain Lady Wingfield.

Except for Smeaton who admitted to bedding the queen (but not to plotting the king's murder), the rest refuted the charges. Norris for one, when confronted with his supposed confession obtained in the Tower, vehemently denied it, saying he was tricked into it by Sir William Fitzwilliam. Nonetheless, he and his co-defendants were all found guilty of 'using fornication with Queen Anne, wife to the king, and also for conspiracy of the king's death', and sentenced to the full horrors of a traitor's death.

It was Anne's turn three days later. As her four so-called lovers had been condemned, her trial was merely a formality: they were guilty, then so was she. Furthermore, by order of the king, Fitzwilliam had broken up her household and let her servants go. Their mistress would not be coming back. But until she was duly condemned and deprived of her title, Anne was still queen, and she proceeded to her judgment in the Great Hall of the Tower with all the dignity and courage she could muster. With her were her attendants, Kingston's wife and her aunt Lady Boleyn, two of the four women assigned to watch over the queen and to take note of her every utterance as to be used as possible evidence against her.

Presiding over the court was the Duke of Norfolk. Despite her being his sister's daughter, Thomas Howard had never liked Anne and considered her arrogant and outspoken. They had often clashed with her using words to him as 'one would address a dog' and him calling her a 'great whore' behind her back. But now it was the duke, not the queen, who occupied the place of honour 'sitting under the Cloth of Estate, representing the king's person as High Steward of England', while his niece was placed before him as a prisoner and defendant. Beneath Norfolk was his son, the Earl of Surrey, holding a golden staff signifying his father's office of Earl Marshal. Close by were twenty-six lords of the realm – including Anne's former lover Henry Percy – who would act as a jury of her peers. Even though Anne as queen had no equal except for the king, they were deemed sufficient to render judgment upon her.

Before some 2,000 spectators, Anne was maligned as a depraved seductress who 'despising the most excellent and noble marriage solemnised between the said Lord our king' and herself, gave way to her 'fickle and carnal appetite' in inviting her paramours, one being her own brother, to her bed. The details of 'foul talk and kisses' between Anne and the four courtiers, and of George Boleyn inserting his tongue into his sister's mouth were so obscene, that one of the judges present noted that 'all the evidence was of bawdry and lechery'.

In her defence, Anne 'made so wise and discreet answers to all things laid against her, excusing herself with her words so clearly as though she had never been faulty to the same'. She denied any intimacy with the men accused with her, especially since she was often not at the places where she was said to have committed the acts. Furthermore, it was unthinkable that she should want her husband dead. Her judges thought otherwise. Knowing that it was the king's wish that his wife be condemned, they found her guilty.

Anne retained her composure, even when the dreadful sentence of

101. Henry Howard, Earl of Surrey. (*By Wenceslaus Hollar after Hans Holbein*)

death was read out – she was to be burnt alive within the Tower on the green or to be beheaded according to 'the king's pleasure'. Before she was led out of the hall, Anne declared that she had not always been as humble and grateful towards the king as she ought to have been, and that she was sorry innocent men were to die because of her. She also asked that she be given time to prepare herself accordingly. But when the court made ready for the trial of Lord Rochford to follow, a sudden recess had to be called for. Henry Percy had fainted. The romantic tradition was that Northumberland had collapsed in distress for convicting his former love, but in fact he was mortally ill. At a meeting of the Order of the Garter held six days later, Percy again suffered 'an unseasonable dizziness of the head, and faintness all over his body'. By the following year, he was dead.

When order was resumed, George Boleyn was brought into court. With his sister found guilty of incest with him, his verdict was almost certainly a foregone conclusion. Still, Rochford put up such a vigorous defence that many said afterwards that 'great money' should have been bet towards his acquittal. But it is unlikely that the viscount could have saved himself as the king was determined to utterly destroy his sister. Perhaps knowing that he would be condemned no matter what, when he was given a note and told not to divulge the embarrassing question aloud

– whether he had been told that Henry VIII was impotent? – Rochford contemptuously disobeyed and read it to the court. His judges found him guilty and Norfolk with tears in his eyes – did he have a soft spot for his nephew? – gave sentence that he, like the other men, be

> hanged, being alive cut down, and then his members cut off and his bowels taken out of his body and burnt before him, and then his head cut off and his body to be divided into four pieces, and his head and body to be set at such places as the king should assign.

Chapter 16

Not only did Henry VIII want his wife dead, but also divorced. He had come to hate Anne as he did Katherine of Aragon, and in his desire to start anew with Jane Seymour, his marriage must be annulled as if it had never existed at all. This would also serve to clear the way for his new family with Jane; already the two were discussing having children together.

On 16 May, Archbishop Cranmer was sent to the Tower to hear Anne's last confession and to get any information from her that could invalidate her union with the king. It remains a mystery what Anne told Cranmer. Perhaps she made a formal acknowledgment that her sister Mary had slept with the king before she did, and thus their marriage was null and void in accordance with religious law. Alternatively, Anne may have stated that she had indeed been formally betrothed to the Earl of Northumberland and in marrying the king afterwards, she had committed bigamy. However, Percy himself had always denied this. He did so in 1532 when his ill-matched wife threatened to make trouble for him and Anne, and again two days before her trial. Upon oath taken at Holy Communion, the earl swore that he be eternally damned 'if ever there were any contract or promise of marriage between her and me'. Still, whatever it was that Anne stated to Cranmer, it was deemed sufficient for him to pronounce that she was 'never lawful Queen of England' at his episcopal palace at Lambeth the following day.

Perhaps it was in hope of life or to protect her family that Anne agreed to the annulment. She later spoke to her wardresses of being exiled to a nunnery and was 'in hope of life'. Had Cranmer promised her this for her cooperation? If he did, Anne had been deceived. On the very day of his visit to the Tower, William Kingston was writing to Thomas Cromwell about the preparations needed for her execution and those of the five men. He had still not been informed whether she was to die by fire or by the axe, and immediate attention needed to be given to Lord Rochford

102. Lambeth Palace. (*By Wenceslaus Hollar*)

and his companions as they were to perish the next day. The earl for one was ready, and his only wish was to 'receive his rites', meaning to hear Mass and take Communion one last time. It was an extraordinary request 'which hath not been used, and in especial here', as Kingston told Cromwell.

Whether Rochford was able to do so or not, he was nonetheless prepared on 17 May. His death warrant and those of his fellow prisoners had been received by Kingston earlier, who then immediately ordered the Tower's carpenter, Master Eretage, to build a scaffold 'of such a height that all present may see it' on Tower Hill. No gallows were erected or a table upon which the victims were to endure the executioner's knife. The king in his mercy had commuted the sentences to mere decapitation. George Boleyn, being the highest in rank, was to die first. Ever the evangelical, he made a speech exhorting the crowd not to be 'discouraged from the Gospel', which had he himself followed more diligently, he exclaimed, he would not be here.

Henry Norris, perhaps out of nervousness, was reported to have said little when it came to his turn. Perhaps the words of William Brereton who followed were what Norris might have intended. Brereton made a general confession of his faults for which he 'deserved to die if it were a thousand deaths', but as to the cause for which he was to suffer, he asked the onlookers to 'judge the best'. It was the expectation that there be no criticism of the law from the condemned, but still, Brereton hinted at the injustice of his sentence. Whether he truly merited his fate, he left that to the people to decide for themselves. Weston also alluded to his past sins for which he had already made amends, he said, but he thought little 'it would have come to this', again implying that he was not guilty. Mark Smeaton, the last to take his place on the scaffold now soaked with blood, simply asked everyone to pray for him as he was worthy of death. His enigmatic plea left the crowd wondering if he meant his adultery with the queen or his lying about it?

Anne herself was set to die on the morning of the 18th. In preparation, she spent much of her remaining time at her devotions with her almoner Skip, and when she took Communion, she asked Kingston to be present as a witness when she made a declaration of her innocence before and after she received the Host. Anne also engaged in conversation with the matrons who watched over her. She had complained to Kingston of their presence, but deprived of all other company, Anne had no choice but to put up with them. When she was later alone with her thoughts, she no doubt made a review of her extraordinary life: how she had reached the greatest heights only to fall in an instant and lose everything, including her very life in the short time to follow. If Anne had any misgivings, it was said that she was remorseful for her treatment of Princess Mary. She was supposedly so contrite that she tearfully begged Lady Kingston to go to her stepdaughter on her behalf and ask her forgiveness. However, the story is apocryphal, and what Anne's feelings of her life spent and misspent were, she kept to herself. Perhaps she hoped that the religious reforms in England would continue even without her, and closer to heart, that her daughter Elizabeth would be well taken care of after she was gone, and that the little girl might even retain a memory of her.

But by the expected hour, no summons came. Anne was then told she was not to die until the afternoon. This short reprieve would have been welcomed by most, but not by Anne. She had prepared herself emotionally and spiritually, and she found the delay upsetting. As the hours passed, Kingston still did not come for her. She was then advised to be ready for the next day. The postponement was not a deliberate attempt to distress Anne in any way, but instead had to do with legalities. Because her death as a treasonous queen was without precedent, the manner of it – by flame or by blade – had to be legally defined and recorded at Westminster, and this was not done until the morning of the 18th. Henry VIII had

103. The White Tower. (*By William Woolnoth after W. Winkle*). The queen's scaffold on Tower Green was built in front of its northern facade shown here.

finally decided that his wife should die by the quicker and more merciful method. On the writ he sent to Kingston, it stated:

> We moved by pity do not wish the same Anne to be committed to be burned by fire. We, however, command … upon the green within our Tower of London aforesaid, the head of the same Anne shall be caused to be cut off.

By the time the order arrived, it was too late to schedule the queen's execution for the day. A scaffold – rather than a stake – still had to be set up, and the Tower had to be cleared of any foreigners so that none could then go overseas with an unfavourable report of the King of England. Kingston suspected that Anne, in her last moments, might publicly declare her innocence and say something unkind about him.

When she was told that she was to indeed die the next day, and by a sword wielded by the famous headsman of Calais, Anne took it in good part. 'I heard say the executioner was very good,' she smiled at Kingston, 'I have a little neck.' She found this most amusing and she 'laughed heartily' as she put her hands about her throat. Later, Anne even made light of herself, how she would soon be called 'Queen Anne the Headless'. Kingston was amazed by her levity. 'I have seen many men and also women executed,' he remarked, 'and all they have been in great sorrow, and to my knowledge this lady has much joy and pleasure in death.'

* * *

On the morning of 19 May, a great crowd gathered by the Lions' Gate, the main entryway into the Tower of London. Even though Kingston had hoped to limit the number of spectators at the queen's execution – which must be done publicly to demonstrate the force of law – by not announcing the day or time, the people had nonetheless been alerted by a procession of the Lord Mayor and the city officials towards the Tower. After they were admitted, some 1,000 persons were also let in to view this extraordinary event. Emotions had run high towards Anne as queen, but after she was arrested and the king seen in the company of Mistress Seymour, there had been a shift in public opinion towards her. While there was still little love for Anne, many people (including Eustace Chapuys) doubted she was guilty of treason as 'few men would believe that she was so abominable'.

By the scaffold built near the White Tower, the officials took their places, along with notables such as the young Duke of Richmond, the Duke of Suffolk, the Earl of Surrey, Thomas Cromwell, and some members of the Council. Unlike the platform built high up for Lord Rochford and the other four on Tower Hill, the one made for Anne upon Tower Green was only about five steps high. The intention was probably so that few could see or hear her as Kingston still worried that she might say something untoward.

At about 8 o'clock, Anne appeared. Behind her were four young ladies in place of the matrons who had formerly been in charge of her. As a concession, Anne was allowed to have her favourites back with her one last time. They had helped their mistress to dress for her final public appearance. Anne wore a robe of black damask and over that, a cape trimmed with ermine. Upon her head was a gable style hood of the 'English fashion'. In her hand, according to tradition, was a book of prayers which she intended to give to one of her attendants.

104. The Execution of Anne Boleyn. (*By an Unknown Artist*)

Anne and her ladies climbed up the scaffold where they immediately caught sight of the masked executioner standing by. If the Frenchman's presence was unnerving to Anne, she did not show it. Instead, following custom, she went towards the edge of the scaffold to say her last words. She had come to submit herself to the law as the law had judged her, she said with a 'smiling countenance', and as to her crimes, God, of whom she asked mercy, knew what they were.

An agent of Lord Lisle who may have been at the Tower that day, described the queen as going to her death 'boldly'. He may simply have meant that she appeared courageous under the terrible circumstances, but maybe there was more to her demeanor. Perhaps there was a defiance to Anne that he could not help but notice. While she did acknowledge the law and even praised the king as protocol demanded of her, she omitted any admission of guilt. She made no confession, and like William Brereton, asked the assembly to make what they will of her offences. 'And if any person will meddle of my cause,' Anne said, 'I require them to judge the best.'

Having made her peace with the world, Anne removed her headdress and replaced it with a linen cap into which her long hair was tucked. After her ladies helped her disrobe, she knelt upon the straw as one of them tied a blindfold over her eyes. The executioner then quietly stepped forward with his sword in hand. As Anne made her prayers aloud, he raised it and in an instant cut her off in mid-sentence.

It was Eustace Chapuys' expectation that Anne's head would be spiked on London Bridge like a common criminal's, but she was spared the indignity. All of her remains were wrapped in a sheet and placed in an elm chest originally used to store arrows. With William Kingston being so preoccupied with arrangements in the past few days, he had apparently forgotten to provide a proper coffin for the queen. It was carried into the little Chapel of Saint Peter Ad Vincula facing Tower Green and deposited into a waiting open grave in the choir which had received George Boleyn earlier. After Anne was laid next to her brother – fitting as he was perhaps the person she had loved most in the world – the flagstones were replaced. No memorial was made to her, and Anne was left to be forgotten and no more spoken of as Henry VIII would have it.

Epilogue

On 15 October 1537, a 'goodly solemnity' was celebrated in the Chapel Royal at Hampton Court. Before a great gathering, a baby was carried to the font to be christened by Archbishop Cranmer. After the ceremonies were all properly performed, the herald proclaimed his name and title, 'Edward, son and heir to the King of England, Duke of Cornwall and Earl of Chester!' After so many years and troubles, Henry VIII had his male successor at last by his new wife, Queen Jane. Among those assembled to honour the child, many were familiar from the time of the king's previous marriage: the Princess Mary, the Dukes of Norfolk and Suffolk, the Marquess of Exeter, Sir Nicholas Carew, Sir Anthony Browne, Sir Nichols Poyntz, Sir Edward Seymour, Sir William Kingston, and Thomas Cromwell.

Curiously, even the Earl of Wiltshire was there. After the fall of his family, Thomas Boleyn was a shadow of his former self. His 'living of late [was] much decayed', as he himself confessed, both emotionally and financially. Two of his children were dead, his wife was ailing, and his relationship with his remaining daughter had yet to be mended. Thomas was further depressed by his ejection from Henry VIII's inner circle. He had been displaced by Edward Seymour as the brother of the new queen, and where once he had been the 'most chiefest' of the Privy Council, and in the king's own estimation, 'knew more of his secret intentions than any other man in the kingdom', it was now Cromwell who had his trust. Thomas even had to surrender his office of Lord Privy Seal to him. It must have been equally galling when Thomas was called upon to participate in the new prince's baptism; he was assigned to bear a 'taper of virgin wax' in the procession. The sight of his granddaughter Elizabeth being carried about in the arms of Edward Seymour must also have been bitter to Thomas. As he looked upon her, perhaps he could not help but think how different it would have all turned out if she had been a boy instead.

Thomas did regain some degree of royal favour when he was reported as being 'very well entertained' at court in January 1538, but his reversal of fortune was short-lived. In April, his wife Elizabeth passed away, and Thomas himself survived her by only less than a year. He died on 12 March 1539. An indication that he was still in the king's good graces in his final months was that Thomas had been allowed to present Henry with a New Year's gift. He gave the king £68 pounds in coin (about £28,650 today) for which he received 'a gilt cup with a cover', 'a gilt cruse with a cover', and 'a gilt salt' in return. When news of Thomas's demise reached court, Henry ordered Requiem Masses to be said for the repose of his soul. It was a final gesture of respect to the man who had once been his father-in-law. Thomas had died peacefully in his bed, but others he knew at the cutthroat court of the Tudors would not be so fortunate. In the remaining years left to Henry VIII and in the succeeding reigns of his children, Edward VI and Mary I, the Marquess of Exeter, Nicholas Carew, Thomas Cromwell, Lady Rochford, the Earl of Surrey, Edward Seymour, and Thomas Cranmer, would all be executed as traitors to the crown.

105. Allegory of the Tudor Succession. (*By an Unknown Artist after Lucas de Heere*)

As for the little girl Thomas Boleyn had no more than fleeting glimpses of at Hampton Court, Elizabeth continued to thrive. Despite her new illegitimacy upon her mother's death, Henry VIII never begrudged her as the daughter of Anne Boleyn, nor did he ever question her paternity. In October 1536, a foreign visitor saw the princess at court with Queen Jane and Princess Mary, and he observed how the king was 'very affectionate' towards her, and 'loves her much'. Before his death in 1547, Henry even restored Elizabeth to the royal succession.

As fate would have it, Elizabeth would eventually wear the crown, but not before various challenges and troubles under her siblings King Edward and Queen Mary. In the time of her sister, Elizabeth would even find herself in the Tower accused of treason as her mother had been. Anne could only have been a distant memory to Elizabeth, but she knew full well of her fall from grace. In reference to her mother, Elizabeth made a request to Mary that should she be killed, might she be dispatched by a sword instead of an axe?

Throughout her long reign, Elizabeth would say little about Anne. Despite her virtual silence, she did honour her memory. At her coronation in 1559, a likeness of 'the right worthy lady Queen Anne' – wearing a crown and holding a sceptre – was given pride of place next to that of Henry VIII in a tableau welcoming Elizabeth to London. As queen, she adopted her mother's falcon badge as her one of her own, and a napkin surviving from the earlier part of her rule bears Anne's coat of arms. That Elizabeth had affection for her mother was evident in Sir William Cecil's choice of a New Year's gift to her. As her principal and most trusted adviser, Cecil was one of the few who knew Elizabeth best, and he would have known what would please her most. In 1563, he presented her with 'a fair book of prayers … silver enamelled, with the queen's and Her Majesty's mother's arms on both sides of gold, garnished and clasped with gold set with garnets and turquoises'. Elizabeth was fond of such luxuries, and another treasure of hers was a locket ring which opened up to reveal miniature portraits of herself and her mother. Aside from such mementos, Elizabeth's regard for Anne was also evident in her relationships to her maternal kin. Although she never got to know her aunt Mary Boleyn (who died in 1543), Elizabeth was close to her cousin Katherine Carey and she valued the service of her brother Henry, whom she later elevated to Baron Hunsdon.

106. The Funeral Procession of Queen Elizabeth. (*By James Basire after William Camden*) The banner with the combined arms of Henry VIII and Anne Boleyn appears in the lower right carried by the queen's kinsman, Baron De La Warr.

The last and the greatest of her family – of both the Boleyns and the Tudors – Elizabeth was much mourned when she died on 24 March 1603. Her funeral was held on 18 April with the queen taken from Whitehall to Westminster Abbey for her final resting place. Tens of thousands had crowded in the streets to see the cortège as it passed. The procession was made up of the queen's household from the lowest to the highest. Except for those who wore ceremonial dress, the rest were attired in deepest black. In the midst was the queen herself. Her casket had been placed on a chariot draped in purple velvet and was driven by four horses in black. On top of it was an effigy of Elizabeth dressed in royal robes, 'having a crown upon her head thereof, and a ball and sceptre in either hand'.

Twelve noblemen, in long hooded cloaks, were given the privilege of walking closest to the late queen. With six on either side of the coffin, each held a banner richly decorated with the escutcheons of Elizabeth's illustrious ancestors. Beginning with those of King Henry II and his wife Eleanor of Aquitaine, the standards fluttered in the wind displaying her proud lineage from the Plantagenets to the Tudors. At the very end were the arms royal of Henry VIII, and impaled with them, the heraldic achievements of Anne Boleyn – honoured once again as Queen of England and as the mother of the great Gloriana.

Notes and Sources

Prologue

Thomas Boleyn's letter to Cromwell is in *L&P*, XI, no. 17.

Chapter 1

For Thomas Boleyn's age: *L & P*, IV, no. 5774, item 14. For the 1507 date for Anne Boleyn, see: Camden, *Annales Rerum Anglicarum et Hibernicarum*, p. 2; Clifford, *The Life of Jane Dormer*, p. 80; Twysden, *An Account of Queen Anne Bullen*, p. 14 and p. 15; and Turner, *The History of England*, X, p. 183, note 6. Twysden's statement that Anne was 'not above seven years of age' when she went to France (in about October 1514) suggests a birth date of sometime after October 1507. For an alternative earlier date: Herbert, *The Life and Reign of King Henry the Eighth*, p. 287; and Paget, 'The Youth of Anne Boleyn'. For possible birthdates of the Boleyn children (with the assumption of 1501 for Anne): Ives, *The Life and Death of Anne Boleyn*, pp. 14–17. If they were born at Blickling, no baptismal records were kept in the parsonage until 1577: Turner, *The History of England*, X, p. 183, note 6. For opposing views that Anne, not Mary, was the elder daughter: Warnicke, *The Rise and Fall of Anne Boleyn*, p. 9, and Mackay, *Among the Wolves at Court*, pp. 25–27. Also, Thomas Lyte's royal pedigree of c. 1605 where Anne is described as 'the eldest da. of Tho. Bullein', reproduced in Doran, *Elizabeth and Mary*, p. 256.

The ghost stories are in Weir, *The Lady in the Tower*, p. 349; and in Strickland, *Lives of the Queens of England*, IV, p. 125. The latter also for Anne's bedroom at Blickling. 'Boleyn', 'Bolleyn', 'Bulleyn', and 'Bullein' as English equivalents of Boulogne are found for example in Hall, *Chronicle*. That Thomas Boleyn may have been at Lincoln's Inn and Cambridge: Mackay, *Among the Wolves at Court*, p. 19. Katherine of Aragon's reception and wedding are described in *The Receyt of the Ladie Kateryne*. For Thomas Boleyn's attendance at the royal wedding and later being called as a witness: *L & P*, IV, no. 5774, item 14. His escorting of Princess Margaret: HMC, *The Manuscripts of His Grace the Duke of Rutland*, I, p. 18.

That Elizabeth Howard supposedly died in 1512 is in Strickland, *Lives of the Queens of England*, IV, p. 125.

Regarding Anne's *Book of Hours*, one example that she had (a work printed in Paris and now at Hever Castle) was known to Katherine of Aragon who owned a copy herself (now in The Morgan Library, New York): McCaffrey, 'Hope from day to day', p. 21. Even though the Boleyn children's education was undocumented, Lord Herbert of Cherbury was certain that music and dancing were an important part: Herbert, *The Life and Reign of King Henry the Eighth*, p. 285. Henry VIII was a skilled musician, as were all his children, Mary, Henry Fitzroy, Elizabeth, and Edward. Princess Mary's reception of the French envoys is in *L&P*, III, no. 896.

For Margaret of Austria's widowhood and her flirtation with Charles Brandon, refer to Nichols, *The Chronicle of Calais*, pp. 68–76. Her bet with Thomas Boleyn is from *L&P*, I, no. 1338.

Chapter 2

Bouton could not have escorted Anne directly from England as his first appearance in the country was not until 1519: Beauvois, *Un Agent Politique de Charles-Quint*, 1st part, p. XXVII. Margaret's letter to Thomas Boleyn is in Le Glay, *Correspondance*, II, p. 461, note 2. An English translation is in Ives, *The Life and Death of Anne Boleyn*, p. 19.

For the placement of Don Diégo's niece, see Le Glay, *Correspondance*, II, pp. 81–82. The Court of Cambrai is discussed in Mareel, *Renaissance Children*, pp. 13–24 and pp. 76–77.

Anne's letter to her father is in Sergeant, *Anne Boleyn*, pp. 275–276. Katherine of Aragon's supposed 'meagre knowledge of French': Paget: 'The Youth of Anne Boleyn', p. 167, note 26. Her French lessons are in *CSP Span.*, I, no. 203 and no. 294. As queen, she was known to have held audiences entirely in French: Hall, *Chronicle*, p. 257. It has been suggested (in Warnicke, *The Rise and Fall of Anne Boleyn*, p. 15) that 'the queen' mentioned in Anne's letter – proposed as being written in the summer of 1514, not 1513 – was Mary Tudor, the queen-to-be of Louis XII. However, Anne's use of the French word '*sage*' ('wise') denotes someone older and experienced such as Katherine of Aragon or Margaret of Austria, rather than the 18-year-old Mary.

Charles of Ghent's accident on Pentecost Monday (26 May 1513) was reported to the emperor in Le Glay, *Correspondance*, II, pp. 155–156. See p. 157 for the Danish envoys.

For the household ordinance incorrectly identifying Anne Boleyn ('Mademoiselle Bullan'), refer to Le Glay, *Correspondance*, II, p. 461, note 2, and Le Baron de Reiffenberg, *Chronique métrique de Chastellain et de Molinet*, p. 154 (but corrected as 'Bulleur' on p. 156). The correct name of Mademoiselle de Bulleux appears in De Quinsonas, *Materiaux pour servir à l'histoire de Marguerite d'Autriche*, III, p. 282, p. 293, p. 295, p. 298, p. 313, and p. 314. Hugues de Bulleux is mentioned in Le Glay, *Correspondance*, II, p. 278.

Anne Boleyn in the schoolroom in the Netherlands, and Anne Brandon and Magdalen Rochester: Warnicke, *The Rise and Fall of Anne Boleyn*, pp. 12–17 and p. 259, note 17. For the *enfants d'honneur*: Mareel, *Renaissance Children*, pp. 19–20.

For Mechelen, refer to Lodovico, *The description of the Low countreys*, p. 50. The Court of Savoy is described in Ives, *The Life and Death of Anne Boleyn*, p. 23; Eichberger, 'A Noble Residence for a Female Regent'; Mareel, *Renaissance Children*, pp. 76–77; and 'Paleis Margaretha van Oostenrijk': https://inventaris.onroerenderfgoed.be/erfgoedobjecten/3472 (accessed December 2021).

Margaret's portraits of Katherine of Aragon and Mary Tudor are mentioned in Eichberger and Beaven, 'Family Members and Political Allies', p. 236. The Horenbouts are discussed in Paget, 'Gerard and Lucas Hornebolt in England'. For composers at the archduchess's court and Anne Boleyn's music book, see Ives, *The Life and Death of Anne Boleyn*, pp. 24–25 and pp. 257–259; and Lowinsky, 'A music book for Anne Boleyn'. Margaret's collection of ethnographic treasures is in MacDonald, 'Collecting a New World'. Of her nieces and nephews, Ferdinand (later Holy Roman Emperor) did not live with her until 1518, while Catherine (later Queen of Portugal) was raised in Spain instead.

Mary of Hungary's later comment about Anne to her brother Ferdinand is in *L & P*, X, no. 965. For the Shrove Tuesday and Ascension Day activities of 1514: Mareel, *Renaissance Children*, p. 20. The Imperial family in La Veure and then in Brussels in 1514 are in Le Glay, *Correspondance*, pp. 254–269. Christian II and Isabeau of Austria's daughter, Christina of Denmark, was later proposed as a fourth wife of Henry VIII.

Mary Tudor's letter to Louis XII is in Sadlack, *The French Queen's Letters*, p. 61. Her choosing of her own husband is on p. 54. Her instruction in French beginning at the age of 2 is on p. 21. Thomas Boleyn's request for Anne is in Sergeant, *Anne Boleyn*, p. 276.

Chapter 3

Mary Tudor's coronation and entry into Paris are described in Ellis, *Original Letters*, Series 2, Vol. 1, pp. 247–254; and Hall, *Chronicle*, p. 571. Her beauty: *CSP Ven.*, II, no. 511.

That Anne probably resided with Renée of France: Warnicke, *The Rise and Fall of Anne Boleyn*, pp 17–18 and pp. 21–22. Their friendship is in Rodocanachi, *Une protectrice de la Réforme en Italie et en France*, pp. 26–27.

King Louis' death is in Holinshed, *Chronicles*, III, p. 610. Mary's complaint about her ladies is quoted in Sadlack, *The French Queen's Letters*, p. 73. Her demand that Brandon marry her is on p. 17. The Brandons' financial penalties to Henry VIII are on p. 115.

Rohan's remark is in Lacroix, *Louis XII et Anne de Bretagne*, p. 306. For the theories behind the Château de Chambord: Tanaka, 'Leonardo da Vinci, Architect of Chambord?'

Francis's quotation is found in De Bourdeille, II, p. x. His denigration of Mary Boleyn is in *L&P*, X, no. 450. For his verses: Sergeant, *Anne Boleyn*, p. 41.

Giustiniani's meeting with the King of England is in *Four Years at the Court of Henry VIII*, I, pp. 90–91. For the English palace at *The Field of the Cloth-of-Gold* and for the event itself: *CSP Ven.*, III, no. 50, no. 69, no. 78, and no. 88. Anne's probable first sight of Henry VIII is in Ives, *The Life and Death of Anne Boleyn*, pp. 25–26. The description of him is from *CSP Ven.*, II, no. 1287. For the Treaty of Bruges and Anne's departure from France: *L&P*, III, no. 1994.

Chapter 4

Anne as being like a Frenchwoman is in Carles, *Épistre*, p. 3. Her books are discussed in Carley, *The Books of King Henry VIII and His Wives*, pp. 124–133. Her reading habits are in Latymer, 'Cronickille of Anne Bulleyne', p. 63, and in Ives, *The Life and Death of Anne Boleyn*, p. 269. The popularity of French culture at the English court is in *CSP Ven.*, II, no. 500. For the king's 'minions': Hall, *Chronicle*, p. 598.

Thomas Wyatt's encounter with Anne at court and her appearance are from George Wyatt's 'Some Particulars of the Life of Queen Anne Boleigne' in Cavendish, *The Life of Cardinal Wolsey*, p. 424. For her looks: Robinson, *Original Letters Relative to the English Reformation*, II, p. 553; *CSP Ven.*, IV, no. 236 and no. 824; Carles, *Épistre*, p. 5; Sander, *Rise and Growth of the Anglican Schism*, p. 25. George Wyatt's biography of Anne as a response to Sander is from Twysden, *An Account of Queen Anne Bullen*, p. 3. Wyatt's poem, slightly modernized here, is taken from Muir, *Collected Poems of Sir Thomas Wyatt*, no. 50, p. 37.

Chapter 5

For the festivities of March 1522: Hall, *Chronicle*, pp. 630–632; *L & P*, III, pp. 1557–1559. Katherine of Aragon's appearance comes from *CSP Ven.*, IV, no. 682. For the belief that Henry Carey was the king's illegitimate son: *L & P*, VIII, no. 567. Mention of Elizabeth Boleyn (and her husband) in royal service is in HMC, *The Manuscripts of His Grace the Duke of Rutland*, I, pp. 21–22. The christening of Frances Brandon is in *L&P*, II, no. 3489.

Anne's affair with Henry Percy is in Cavendish, *The Life of Cardinal Wolsey*, pp. 120–129. Henry VIII's supposed first meeting with Anne is from Leti, *La Vie d'Elizabeth Reine D'Angleterre*, p. 48. The king's letters to Anne are transcribed in Ridley, *The Love Letters of Henry VIII*, pp. 35–71. His dislike of writing is in *L & P*, III, no. 1. For Anne's possible reaction to being courted according to Marie Louise Bruce: Jones, 'The story of a king's lust that changed history', p. 5. Praise of the new king comes from Allen, *Opus Epistolarum*, I, no. 215. Henry Fitzroy's elevation is in *CSP Ven.*, III, no. 1053.

Chapter 6

Katherine's belief that Wolsey was plotting against her is in Hall, *Chronicle*, p. 756.

Pole's denunciation of Anne is from his *Defense of the Unity of the Church*, p. 185. But Anne as 'the first origin of the whole lying affair' as sometimes quoted is a misreading; Pole was referring to Archbishop Cranmer. The correct translation is on p. 186. The dismissal of Anne's character was by Agnes Strickland, *Lives of the Queens of England*, IV, p. 122.

Regarding Thomas Boleyn's ambitions for Anne, Chapuys' statement (derived from the unfriendly Duke of Norfolk) that he was against her being queen is suspicious: *CSP Span.*, IV (ii), no. 1048 and 1077. His more believable reaction is in Cavendish, *The Life of Cardinal Wolsey*, p. 427.

Anne's gift to the king and his responses are in Ridley, *The Love Letters of Henry VIII*, p. 43 and p. 65.

The entertaining of the French envoys is in Lingard, *The History of England*, IV, p. 237 and *CSP Ven.*, IV, no. 105. For the annulment the royal marriage, see *CSP Span.*, III (ii), no. 69 and no. 113. Charles V's response is in *CSP Span.*, III (ii), no. 131. The pillaging of Rome is given in *CSP Span.*, III (ii), no. 70.

Chapter 7

The king and Wolsey's attempts to win support: *L&P*, IV, no. 3231. For Knight's secret mission: *L&P*, IV, no. 3422. Wolsey's cool reception at home is in *CSP Span.*, III (ii), no. 224. For Gardiner and Fox's meeting with Clement VII: *L&P*, IV, no. 4090.

For the sweating sickness, refer to *L&P*, IV, no. 4656, no. 4305, and no. 4408.

Katherine's attitude towards Anne is in Cavendish, *The Life of Cardinal Wolsey*, p. 131 and p. 428. Wolsey's gifts to Anne are in *L&P*, IV, no. 4005. Her new lodgings and her meeting with Fox are mentioned in Pocock, *Records of the Reformation*, I, p. 141–142. See also Thurley, *Houses of Power*, pp. 99–101, for her accommodations at Greenwich.

The disagreement over the nuns is in Ridley, *Love Letters*, p. 59; *L&P*, IV, no. 4488, no. 4497, no. 4507, and no. 4509.

Chapter 8

Anne's absence from court comes from *CSP Span.*, III (ii), no. 541. The request to Margaret of Austria for jurists is in *State Papers, King Henry the Eighth*, VII, pp. 115–116. Henry's reaction to her death is in *CSP Span.*, IV (ii), no. 584. The couple's plans to be wed are mentioned in *CSP Span.*, III (ii), no. 550. For the coming of the papal legate: Ridley, *Love Letters*, p. 45. His arrival is in *CSP Ven.*, IV, no. 374. Campeggio's efforts to win over the queen and his meeting with her are in *L&P*, IV, no. 4875. The trial at Blackfriars is described in *CSP Ven.*, IV, no. 482, and in Cavendish, *The Life of Cardinal Wolsey*, p. 211–218. The depositions about Katherine's wedding night are in *L&P*, IV, no. 5774. The adjournment of the court is described in Cavendish, *The Life of Cardinal Wolsey*, pp. 229–233.

Chapuys' opinions of Anne's religion: *CSP Span.*, IV (ii), no. 664; *CSP Span.*, V (ii), no. 43. For Simon Fish and his controversial tract, see his *A Supplication for the Beggars*. For Tyndale, refer to: Strype, *Ecclesiastical Memorials*, I (i), pp. 171–172.

Chapter 9

Anne's prominence at court is described in *L&P*, IV, no. 5016. Wolsey's letter to Cromwell is in *State Papers, King Henry the Eighth*, I, pp. 351–352. For the plotting against him: *CSP Span.*, IV (i), no. 132. Wolsey's fall is reported in Hall, *Chronicle*, p. 774; *CSP Span.*, IV (i), no. 194 (here also for praise of Thomas More). Wolsey's lament is in Cavendish, *The Life of Cardinal Wolsey*, p. 387.

The queen's sadness is given in *CSP Span.*, IV (i), no. 83. For Chapuys as the new ambassador: *CSP Span.*, IV (i), no. 57. As the queen's 'especial friend': *CSP Span.*, V (i), no. 134. Anne's high living is in Cavendish, *The Life of Cardinal Wolsey*, p. 130. For the royal couple's arguments at dinner: *CSP Span.*, V (i), no. 182 and no. 224.

Dislike of Anne is described in Hall, *Chronicle*, p. 759. Her defiance is in *CSP Span.*, IV (ii), no. 584; *CSP Span.*, IV (i), no. 547. For Thomas Cranmer's advice on the divorce: Foxe, *Acts and Monuments*, VIII, pp. 6–9. Thomas Cromwell's early years are in Foxe, *Acts and Monuments*, V, p. 392. His sadness for Wolsey is in Cavendish, *The Life of Cardinal Wolsey*, pp. 259–260. More's advice to him comes from Roper, *The Life of Sir Thomas More*, pp. 68–69.

The submission of the clergy is in Hall, *Chronicle*, p. 774. The decisions of the universities and the queen's reaction are in Hall, *Chronicle*, pp. 775–781. Anne's quarrel with Henry Guildford is in *CSP Span.*, IV (ii), no. 739. Her fight with the king is from *CSP Span.*, IV (ii), no. 608. Her dominance over him is in *CSP Ven.*, IV, no. 682. The abandonment of the queen is in Hall, *Chronicle*, p. 781.

Chapter 10

For the splendour of The More: Pollard, *Wolsey*, p. 325. Katherine's exile there is described in CSP Ven., IV, no. 682. For Anne's new state: *CSP Span.*, IV (ii), no. 880. The building projects at Whitehall and Hampton Court are described in Thurley, *Houses of Power*, pp. 123–126 and pp. 172–173.

The book of prophecies comes from Wyatt, 'Some Particulars of the Life of Queen Anne Boleigne', pp. 429–430.

Anne's elevation as Marquess of Pembroke is in *L&P*, V, no. 1274; *CSP Ven.*, IV, no. 802; *CSP Span.*, IV (ii), no. 993. The demand for Katherine's jewels, Anne supposedly to be married in Calais, and the problem of who to receive her are all in *CSP Span.*, IV (ii), no. 1003. For the refurbishment of the Tower that autumn: *CSP Span.*, IV (ii), no. 993.

The meeting with King Francis is described in 'The manner of the triumph at Calais and Boulogne' in *An English Garner*, II, pp. 33–40; *Cal. Marquis of Bath*, IV, pp. 1–12; Hall, *Chronicle*, p. 789–794. Among those also going to Calais were Thomas Cromwell, Nicholas Poyntz, William Kingston, William Brereton, Henry Norris, Richard Page, Francis Weston, and Mark Smeaton. Francis I had been forced to wed Charles V's sister as a condition of his release after he was captured by Imperial forces at the Battle of Pavia in 1525.

Chapter 11

Details of the secret marriage are in Sander, *Rise and Growth of the Anglican Schism*, p. 94; *CSP Span.*, IV (ii), no. 1053; *L&P*, VI, no. 661. Hall, *Chronicle*, p. 794 gives a different wedding date of 14 November 1532. Perhaps the couple did have an earlier ceremony or a formal betrothal.

Anne's wish to go on a pilgrimage and her encounter with Wyatt is in Friedmann, *Anne Boleyn*, I, pp. 189–190. For Henry VIII at Walsingham: Spelman, *The English Works of Sir Henry Spelman*, II, p. 149. Anne and Henry's hint dropping about their marriage is in Friedmann, *Anne Boleyn*, I, pp. 189–190; *CSP Span.*, IV (ii), no. 1055. For the valuable plate: Thurley, *Houses of Power*, pp. 129–130. Anne as queen that Easter is from *CSP Span.*, IV (ii), no. 1061. Cranmer's pronouncement in favour of the king is in *L&P*, VI, no. 528, no. 529, and no. 531. For Katherine's defiance, see *CSP Span.*, IV (ii), no. 1061.

Anne's coronation comes from *L&P*, VI, no. 563 and no. 584; Hall, *Chronicle*, pp. 798–805; 'The Noble Triumphant Coronation of Queen Anne – Wife Unto the Most Noble King Henry VIII' in Arber, *An English Garner*, II, pp. 41–60. The confiscation of Katherine's barge is in *CSP Span.*, IV (ii), no. 556. The repairs to the Tower are given in Keay, *The Elizabethan Tower of London*, pp. 28, 41, and 43–45; Thurley, *Houses of Power*, pp. 127–130.

For the comet of 1533, see: *CSP Ven.*, IV, no. 956; *L&P*, VI, no. 888; *CSP Span.*, IV (ii), no. 1004; Kokott, 'The Comet of 1533'. For Halley's Comet of 1066: William of Malmesbury; *The History of the Kings of England*, p. 288. My thanks to Dr. Martin Spies (Justus Liebig University Giessen) for his help regarding the 1533 Prueckner image. For the comet of 1532: *CSP Span.*, IV (ii), no. 1004; *CSP Ven.*, IV, no. 816. Refer to the latter for the portents as well, along with *L&P*, VI, no. 1466. For Henry and Anne's happiness: *L&P*, VI, no. 879; *L&P*, VIII, no. 919 (misdated as June 1535).

The merriment among the queen's ladies is in *L&P*, VI, no. 613. That the king was divinely inspired to marry her: *CSP Ven.*, IV, no. 924. The preparations for the birth and the pair's quarrel are in *CSP Span.*, IV (ii), no. 1123. The slander against the king is in *L&P*, VI, no. 1065.

The regulations for Anne's confinement are provided by Leland, *Collectanea*, IV, pp. 179–180. For the birth of the child: *L&P*, VI, no. 1111.

Chapter 12

Reactions to the princess's birth are in *CSP Span.*, IV (ii), no. 1124 and no. 1127. The christening is described in Hall, *Chronicle*, pp. 805–806. Anne's demand for the cloth is in *CSP Span.*, IV (ii), no. 1107. Henry's continuing love for Anne is in *CSP Span.*, IV (ii), no. 1144 and in *L&P*, VI, no. 1293. For her churching, see Warnicke, *The Rise and Fall of Ane Boleyn*, p. 168. Henry's previous optimism is in Giustinian, *Four Years at the Court of Henry VIII*, I, pp. 181–182. For Elizabeth's delivery and her appearance: Carles, *Épistre*, pp. 8–9.

For the Christmases at the royal court: Hall, *Chronicle* p. 803 and p. 784. Also: Stow, *The Survey of London*, p. 98. Gift giving was celebrated according to the Roman calendar with New Year's Day being on 1 January (as opposed to 25 March – Lady Day – as was observed in England). The Italian description of Henry VIII is found in *CSP Ven.*, IV, no. 682. For the 1534 New Year's gifts: *L&P*, VII, no. 9. See also Ives, 'The Queen and the painters', pp. 37–38 for the fountain, and Hayward, 'Gift Giving at the Court of Henry VIII', p. 158 and p. 171 for Jane Seymour. Anne's gifts to her ladies are mentioned in *L&P*, VI, no. 1194 and no. 1589.

For Anne being pregnant in 1534: *L&P*, VII, no. 556. The 1534 medal is now in the British Museum (inventory M.9010). The damage appears to have occurred between the late 19th to early 20th century: Hui, 'The Modern Day Mystery of Anne Boleyn's 1534 Medal', *Tudor Faces Blog* (July 2021): https://tudorfaces.blogspot.com/2021/07/the-modern-day-mystery-of-anne-boleyns.html (accessed December 2021). That the medal was a royal commission: Ives *The Life and Death of Anne Boleyn*, pp. 41–42. A modern recreation of it has been created by sculptor Lucy Churchill: www.lucychurchill.com/anne-boleyn-moost-happi-medal-reconstruction/ (accessed December 2021).

For the *Black Book of the Garter*: Hui, 'Anne Boleyn as 'The Lady of the Garter': A Rediscovered Image of Henry VIII's Second Queen', *Tudor Faces Blog*, (April 2017):

https://tudorfaces.blogspot.com/2017/04/anne-boleyn-as-lady-of-garter.html (accessed December 2021).

Chapuys' reporting of the miscarriage is in *CSP Span.*, V (i), no. 90. The proposed meeting with Francis I is in *L&P*, VII, no. 958. The silver cradle is mentioned in *L&P*, VII, no. 1668. The couple's quarrel is from *CSP Span.*, V (i), no. 90.

190 Anne Boleyn

For Mary Boleyn's secret marriage and pregnancy: *CSP Span.*, V (i), no. 118; Wood, *Letters of Royal and Illustrious Ladies of Great Britain*, II. pp. 193–197. A report that Mary Boleyn was with her sister in January 1536 may be dubious: *L&P*, X, no. 450.

The insults against Anne are given in *L&P*, VI, no. 1254 and no. 585; *L&P*, VIII, no. 196. For the Act of Succession: *The Statutes of the Realm*. III, pp. 471–474. The Nun of Kent's prophecies are in *L&P*, VI, no. 1466. Those of Elizabeth Amadas: *L&P*, VI, no. 923. That a woman would bring disaster to England: *CSP Span.*, IV (i), no. 547. For Merlin foretelling Anne's doom: *L&P*, X, no. 911.

Princess Mary's defiance is in *CSP Span.*, IV (ii), no. 1143; *CSP Span.*, V (i), no. 22 and no. 68.

For Chabot at the English court: *CSP Span.*, V (i), no. 112, no. 114, and no. 118. Anne's confiding in Gontier is in *L&P*, VIII, no. 174.

Chapter 13

For the progress of 1535, particularly the stopover at Acton Court: Starkey, *Henry VIII: A European Court in England*, pp. 118–125; Leland, *Itinerary*, VII, p. 101; *L&P*, VIII, no. 989. The intention was to go as far as Bristol, but an outbreak of plague prevented them from actually entering the city: Starkey, *Six Wives*, pp. 530–531.

Henry VIII's exuberance is given in *CSP Span.*, V (i), no. 181. The execution of the Carthusian monks is in *L&P*, VIII, no. 895. The anti-clerical play is mentioned in *CSP Span.*, V (i), no. 179. The king and queen as merry together: *L&P*, IX, no. 525.

Anne's affection for Margaret of Angoulême is in *L&P*, IX, no. 378; Twysden, *An Account of Queen Anne Boleyn*, p. 15. Praise for Anne's religious activities comes from Foxe, *Acts and Monuments*, V, p. 135; Aylmer, *An Harborowe For Faithful and Trewe Subjectes*, unpaginated. For the books by d'Etaples: Carley, *The Books of King Henry VIII and His Wives*, pp. 125–131; Ives, *The Life and Death of Anne Boleyn*, pp. 271–272. Anne's aiding of Thomas Forman (or his associate Thomas Garrett) is in *L&P*, IV, Appendix, no. 197; Cooper et al, *Athenae Cantabrigienses*, I. p. 37. For Thomas Alwaye: Dowling, *Anne Boleyn and Reform*, p. 30. Anne's protection of the French woman and Bourbon: Latymer, *Cronickille of Anne Bulleyne*, p. 56. Bourbon's gratitude is in Ives, *The Life and Death of Anne Boleyn*, p. 275. Anne's scholastic patronages are in Latymer, *Cronickille of Anne Bulleyne*, p. 57; Dowling, *Anne Boleyn and Reform*, p. 34.

Anne's admonition to her servants and mention of the Bibles are in Latymer, *Cronickille of Anne Bulleyne*, pp. 62–63; Starkey, *Henry VIII*, p. 109. The visit to Syon and the holy relic are in Latymer, *Cronickille of Anne Bulleyne*, pp. 60–61. See also 'The Holy Blood of Hailes' in 'History and Stories': www.english-heritage.org.uk/visit/places/hailes-abbey/history-and-stories/the-holy-blood-of-hailes/ (accessed December 2021).

Chapter 14

The reactions to Katherine's death are in *CSP Span.*, V (ii), no. 9 and no. 13. See also Hall, *Chronicle*, p. 818. Her wish not to die alone is in *CSP Span.*, V (ii), no. 3. For Maria de Salinas: Strype, *Ecclesiastical Memorials*, I, part 1, p. 372.

Chapuys' machinations are in *CSP Span.*, V (i), no. 45. Katherine's refusal to condone violence is in *CSP Span.*, V (i), no. 1. Chapuys' meeting with Cromwell and his visit to court is in *CSP Span.*, V (ii), no. 43a. For the emperor's demands: *State Papers, King Henry the Eighth*, VII, pp. 683–688.

The king's jousting accident is in *L&P*, X, no. 200; Wriothesley, *Chronicle*, I, p. 33. Anne's miscarriage is in *CSP Span.*, V (ii), no. 21.

For Henry VIII's courting of Jane Seymour: *CSP Span.*, V (ii), no. 21. Her looks are noted in *L&P*, X, no. 901. Her refusal of the king's gift and her working against Anne are in *CSP Span.*, V (ii), no. 43. Anne's mistreatment of Jane is in Clifford, *Life of Jane Dormer*, p. 79.

Thomas Boleyn's election to the Garter is described in Anstis et al,, *Register*, I, pp. 360–361. For Carew, see pp. 400–401. Refer to *CSP Span.*, V (ii), no. 47 for the Boleyns' disappointment.

For Luther's praise of Cromwell, see: Doran, *Henry VIII*, p. 167. Anne's opposition to him is proposed by Ives, *The Life and Death of Anne Boleyn*, pp. 307–312. Her threat and Cromwell's worries are in *CSP Span.*, V (ii), no. 43.

The trip to Dover is mentioned in *L&P*, X, no. 673. Elizabeth at Hatfield House: Strickland, *Lives of the Queens of England*, VI, pp. 8–9. Anne's expenses for her are in *L&P*, X, no. 913. For Matthew Parker in Anne's service: Dowling, *Anne Boleyn and Reform*, p. 40.

Anne Boleyn's conversation with Norris is from *L&P*, X, no. 793. Her appeal to Henry VIII is in *CSP For.*, I, no. 1303.

For Holbein's *King Solomon and the Queen of Sheba* as representations of Henry VIII and Anne Boleyn: Ives, *The Life and Death of Anne Boleyn*, pp. 235–236; Ives, 'The Queen and the painters', p. 39.

Chapter 15

For the May Day jousts: Wriothesley, *Chronicle*, I, p. 35. For Anne's arrest and imprisonment, and those accused with her: *L&P*, X, no. 793, no. 797, no. 798, no. 890, no. 902, and no. 910; Wriothesley, *Chronicle*, I, p. 36; Constantine, *A Memorial*, p. 64. Anne's difficulty in getting a letter to Cromwell and Kingston's lack of mention of one to the king, suggests that the letter supposedly written by

Anne to Henry VIII from the Tower (*L&P*, X, no. 808) is dubious. Shaxton's denunciation is in *L&P*, X, no. 942. Cranmer's letter is in *L&P*, X, no. 792.

Lady Rochford's plea to Cromwell is in: Ellis, *Original Letters*, 1st series, II, CXXIV. For Henry VIII's reaction and Chapuys' remark: *CSP Span.*, V (ii), no. 55 and *CSP Span.*, V (ii), no. 61 (for a different translation), and also *Span.*, V (ii), no. 54.

Cromwell's move against Anne is in *CSP Span.*, V (ii), no. 61.

Lady Worcester's accusation is described in Carles, *Épistre*, pp. 14–17. For the identification of her and her brother: Ives, *The Life and Death of Anne Boleyn*, pp. 332–333. For the trials: Wriothesley, *Chronicle*, pp. 36–39 and Appendix; Constantine, *A Memorial*, p. 64–66; *CSP Span.*, V (i), no. 55; Spelman, *Reports*, I. p. 71; Carles, *Épistre*, pp. 26–37. See also *L&P*, V, no. 12 for Lady Wingfield.

Anne and Norfolk's mutual dislike is in *CSP Span.*, V (i), no. 122. Percy's illness is mentioned in Anstis et al, *Register*, I, pp. 401–402 and in *L&P*, X, no. 715.

Chapter 16

Henry and Jane's plans to have children together are in *CSP Span.*, V (ii), no. 55.

For the annulment of Anne's marriage: Friedmann, *Anne Boleyn*, I. pp.159–161; *L&P*, X, no. 864; Wriothesley, *Chronicle*, pp. 40–41. Her hope of life and the preparations for the executions: *L&P*, X, no. 890. The deaths of the five men are in Constantine, *A Memorial*, p. 65.

Anne's affirmation of her innocence is in *L&P*, X, no. 910; *CSP Span.*, V (ii), no. 55. Her supposed regret over Princess Mary is in Strickland, *Lives of the Queens of England*, IV, pp. 205–206. See also: *L&P*, X, no. 1070, but Chapuys may have reported this to please the emperor.

For the manner of Anne's death: 'How to kill a queen? Preparing for the execution of Anne Boleyn in May 1536', *The National Archives*, 25 November 2020: https://blog.nationalarchives.gov.uk/how-to-kill-a-queen-preparing-for-the-execution-of-anne-boleyn-in-may-1536/ (accessed December 2021).

The events of 18 May at the Tower are described in *L&P*, X, no. 910. Anne's joke about herself is in *L&P*, X, no. 1070. Her execution is described in Wriothesley, *Chronicle*, pp. 41–42; Hall, *Chronicle*, p. 819; Thomas, *The Pilgrim*, pp. 116–117; Bentley, *Excerpta Historica*, pp. 264–265; *CSP Span.*, V (ii), no. 55; *L&P*, X, no. 919 and 920; Constantine, *A Memorial*, pp. 65–66. The executioner's fee is given in *L&P*, XI, no. 381. The Duke of Richmond, present at the execution, would die in July 1536 of an illness.

Epilogue

Prince Edward's baptism is described in Wriothesley, *Chronicle*, pp. 67–68; *L&P*, XII (ii), no. 911. Thomas Boleyn's reduced living is mentioned in *L&P*, XI, no.

17. That his wife may have been suffering from tuberculosis: Mackay, *Among the Wolves at Court*, p. 217. Here also on pp. 223–224 that Thomas may have later reconciled with his daughter Mary. His former high status is mentioned in Cavendish: *The Life of Cardinal Wolsey*, p. 119 and *CSP Span.*, IV (i), no. 250. His return to court: *L&P*, XIII (i), no. 24. His final gift giving with the king is in Hayward, 'Gift Giving at the Court of Henry VIII', p. 145 and p. 164. The Requiem Masses are mentioned in *L&P*, XIV (i), no. 950.

Henry VIII's affection for Elizabeth is in *L&P*, XI, no. 860. Her request for a death by the sword is in Castelnau, *Mémoires*, p. 289. Her mentions of Anne: Jenkins, *Elizabeth the Great*, pp. 15–16. The tableau with Henry and Anne is in Nichols, *The Progresses and Public Processions*, II, p. 41.

For Elizabeth honouring Anne's memory: Hui, 'Queen Elizabeth's Napkin', *Tudor Faces Blog* (June 2013): https://tudorfaces.blogspot.com/2013/06/queen-elizabeths-napkin.html (accessed December 2021).

Cecil's gift to the queen is listed in Colthorpe, 'The Elizabethan Court Day by Day', *Folgerpedia*, for the year 1563: https://folgerpedia.folger.edu/The_Elizabethan_Court_Day_by_Day (accessed December 2021).

The locket ring is described in Doran, *Elizabeth*, pp. 12–13. It should also be mentioned that in a painting of Henry VIII and his family (Royal Collection RCIN 405796), a teenage Elizabeth is shown wearing a letter *A* pendant; probably a jewel associated with her late mother.

The description of Elizabeth's funeral comes from Stow and Howes, *Annales*, p. 815. For the heraldic banners: Niccols, *Expicedium*, unpaginated. Henry and Anne's standard was carried by Thomas West, Baron De La Warr, a great-grandson of Mary Boleyn, after whom the American state of Delaware was later named after.

Bibliography

Allen, P. S. (editor), *Opus Epistolarum Des. Erasmi Roterodami*, Oxford: Henry Frowde, 1906.
Anstis, J. et al., *The Register of the Most Noble Order of the Garter*, London: printed by John Barber, 1724.
Arber, Edward (editor), *An English Garner: Ingatherings from our History and Literature*, Westminster: Archibald Constable & Co., 1845.
Aylmer, John, *An Harborowe For Faithful and Trewe Subjectes*, Strasbourg, 1559.
Astor, Gavin (Second Baron Astor of Hever), *Hever Castle and Gardens: History and Guide*, Norwich: Jarrold & Sons, 1977.
Beauvois, M. E., *Un Agent Politique de Charles-Quint: Le Bourguignon Claude Bouton, Seigneur de Corberon*, Paris: Société d'histoire, etc., de Beaune, 1882.
Bentley, Samuel, *Excerpta Historica or Illustrations of English History*, London, 1831.
Bourdeille, Pierre de, *Lives of Fair and Gallant Ladies*, (translated by Alfred Richard Allinson), London: The Alexandrian Society, Inc., 1922.
Bruce, Marie Louise, *Anne Boleyn*, New York: Coward, McCann & Geoghegan, 1972.
Calendar of Letters, Despatches, and State Papers Relating to the Negotiations between England and Spain Preserved in the Archives at Simancas and Elsewhere (CSP Span.), (edited by G.A. Bergenroth, Pascual de Gayangos, M. A. S. Hume, & R. Tyler), London: Longman, Green, Longman, & Roberts, 1862–1954.
Calendar of State Papers and Manuscripts Relating to English Affairs Existing in the Archives and Collections of Venice (CSP Ven.), (edited by Rawdon Brown et al.), London: Longman, Green, Reader, & Dyer; also H.M.S.O., 1864–1947.
Calendar of the Manuscripts of the Marquis of Bath Preserved at Longleat, Wiltshire (Cal. Marquis of Bath), Dublin: H.M.S.O., 1907–1968.
Camden, William, *Annales Rerum Anglicarum et Hibernicarum regnante Elizabetha ad annum salutis M.D.LXXXIX*, London, 1615.
Castelnau, Michel de, *Mémoires*, Paris, 1794.
Cavendish, George, *The Life of Cardinal Wolsey* (edited by S.W. Singer), second edition, London: Printed by Thomas Davison for Harding & Lepard, 1827.
Carles, Lancelot de, *Épistre contenant le procès criminel faict à l'encontre de la royne Anne Boullant d'Angleterre*, Lyon, 1545.
Carley, James P., *The Books of King Henry VIII and His Wives*, London: The British Library, 2004.
Chapman, Hester W., *Anne Boleyn*, London: Jonathan Cape, 1974.
Clifford, Henry, *The Life of Jane Dormer, Duchess of Feria*, (transcribed by Canon E.E. Estcourt & edited by Rev. Joseph Stevenson), London: Burns & Oates Limited, 1887.
Constantine, George, 'A Memorial from George Constantine to Thomas Lord Cromwell', (edited by T. Amyot), *Archaeologia*, 23 (1831), London: Society of Antiquaries of London, pp. 50–78.
Cooper, Charles Henry; Cooper, Thompson; Gray, George John, *Athenae Cantabrigienses*, Cambridge: Deighton, Bell & Co. & Macmillan & Co., 1858.
Doran, Susan (editor), *Elizabeth: The Exhibition at the National Maritime Museum*, London: Chatto & Windus, 2003.

Doran, Susan (editor), *Elizabeth and Mary: Royal Cousins, Rival Queens*, London: The British Library, 2021.
Doran, Susan (editor), *Henry VIII: Man & Monarchy,* London: The British Library, 2009.
Dowling, Maria, 'Anne Boleyn and Reform', *The Journal of Ecclesiastical History*, 35 (1984), pp. 30–46.
Eichberger, Dagmar, 'A Noble Residence for a Female Regent: Margaret of Austria and the "Court of Savoy" in Mechelen', *Architecture and the Politics of Gender in Early Modern Europe*, (edited by Helen Hills), Burlington: Routledge, 2003, pp. 25–46.
Eichberger, Dagmar & Beaven, Lisa, 'Family Members and Political Allies: The Portrait Collection of Margaret of Austria', *The Art Bulletin*, Vol. 77, No. 2 (June 1995), pp. 225–248.
Ellis, Henry, *Original Letters Illustrative of English History*, London: printed for Harding, Triphook, & Lepard, 1824.
Fish, Simon, *A Supplication for the Beggars*, (edited by Edward Arber), Westminster: Archibald Constable & Co., 1895.
Foxe, John, *Acts and Monuments*, (edited by Stephen Reed Cattley), London: R.B. Seeley & W. Burnside, 1837–1841.
Friedmann, Paul, *Anne Boleyn: A Chapter of English History, 1527–1536,* London: Macmillan & Co., 1884.
Giustinian, Sebastian, *Four Years at the Court of Henry VIII*, (edited & translated by Rawdon Brown), London: Smith, Elder, & Co., 1854.
Hall, Edward, *Hall's Chronicle; Containing the History of England, During the Reign of Henry the Fourth and the Succeeding Monarchs*, London: printed for J. Johnson, 1809.
Hayward, Maria, 'Gift Giving at the Court of Henry VIII: The 1539 New Year's Gift Roll in Context', *The Antiquaries Journal*, Vol. 85, September 2005, pp. 126–175.
Herbert, Edward (Lord Herbert of Cherbury), *The Life and Reign of King Henry the Eighth*, London: printed by Mary Clark for Ann Mearn, 1683.
Historical Manuscripts Commission (HMC), *The Manuscripts of His Grace the Duke of Rutland G.C.B., Preserved at Belvoir Castle*, London: His Majesty's Stationery Office, 1888 (reissued 1911).
Holinshed, Raphael, *Chronicles of England, Scotland, and Ireland*, London: printed for J. Johnson et al., 1808.
Ives, E. W., *The Life and Death of Anne Boleyn*, Oxford: Blackwell Publishing, 2004.
Ives, E. W., 'The Queen and the painters: Anne Boleyn, Holbein and Tudor royal portraits', *Apollo*, July 1994, No. 140, pp. 36–45.
Jenkins, Elizabeth, *Elizabeth the Great*, New York: Coward-McCann, Inc., 1959.
Jones, Frank, 'The story of a king's lust that changed history', *The Montreal Gazette*, 25 May 1981, p. 1 and p. 5.
Keay, Anna, *The Elizabethan Tower of London: The Haiward and Gascoyne Plan of 1597*, London: London Topographical Society, 2001.
Kokott, Wolfgang, 'The Comet of 1533', *Journal for the History of Astronomy*, Vol. 12, 1981, pp. 95–112.
Lacroix, Paul, *Louis XII et Anne de Bretagne: chronique de l'histoire de France*, Paris: Georges Hurtrel, 1882.
Latymer, William, 'Cronickille of Anne Bulleyne,' (edited by Maria Dowling), *Camden Miscellany*, XXX, 4th series, 39, 1990.
Le Glay, M., *Correspondance de l'empereur Maximilien Ier et de Marguerite d'Autriche, sa fille, gouvernante des Pays-Bas, de 1507 à 1519, publiée d'après les Manuscrits originaux*, Paris: Jules Renouard et Cie., 1839.
Leland, John, *Antiquarii Rebus Britannicis Collectanea*, (edited by Thomas Hearne), London, 1770.

Leland, John, *The Itinerary of John Leland, The Antiquary*, (edited by Thomas Hearne), Oxford, 1769.
Leti, Gregorio, *La Vie d'Elizabeth Reine D'Angleterre*, Amsterdam: Henry Desbordes, 1714.
Letters and Papers, Foreign and Domestic, of the Reign of Henry VIII (L&P), (edited by J.S. Brewer), London: Longmans, H.M.S.O., 1862–1910.
Lingard, John, *The History of England, From the first Invasion by the Romans to the Accession of William and Mary in 1688*, London: Charles Dolman, 1855.
Lodovico, Guicciardini, *The description of the Low countreys and of the prouinces thereof, gathered into an epitome out of the historie of Lodouico Guicchardini*, (edited by Thomas Danett), London: by Peter Short for Thomas Chard, 1593.
Lofts, Norah, *Anne Boleyn*, New York: Coward, McCann & Geoghegan, Inc., 1979.
Lowinsky, Edward E., 'A music book for Anne Boleyn', *Florilegium Historiale*, (edited by J.G. Rowe & W.H. Stockdale), Toronto, 1971, pp. 160–235.
MacDonald, Deanna, 'Collecting a New World: The Ethnographic Collections of Margaret of Austria', *The Sixteenth Century Journal*, Autumn, 2002, Vol. 33, No. 3, pp. 649–663.
Mackay, Lauren, *Among the Wolves at* Court: *The Untold Story of Thomas and George Boleyn*, New York: I.B. Tauris, 2018.
Mareel, Samuel (editor), *Renaissance Children: Art and Education at the Hapsburg Court (1480–1530)*, Tielt: Lannoo Publishers, 2021.
McCaffrey, Kate E., 'Hope from day to day: Inscriptions newly discovered in a book owned by Anne Boleyn', *The Times Literary Supplement*, 21 May 2021, p. 21.
Muir, Kenneth (editor), *Collected Poems of Sir Thomas Wyatt*, London: Routledge & Kegan Paul Ltd., 1949.
Niccols, Richard, *Expicedium, A Funeral Oration Upon the Death of the Late Deceased Princess of Famous Memorye, Elizabeth by the Grace of God, Queen of England, France and Ireland*, London: Edward Allde, 1603.
Nichols, John Gough (editor), *The Chronicle of Calais, in the Reigns of Henry VII and Henry VIII*, London: The Camden Society, 1846.
Nichols, John Gough, *The Progresses and Public Processions of Queen Elizabeth*, London: John Nichols & Son, 1823.
Paget, Hugh, 'Gerard and Lucas Hornebolt in England', *The Burlington Magazine*, 101, November 1959, pp. 396–402.
Paget, Hugh, 'The Youth of Anne Boleyn', *Bulletin of The Institute of Historical Research*, Vol. 54, Issue 130, 1981, pp. 162–170.
Pocock, Nicholas, *Records of the Reformation: The Divorce 1527–1533*, Oxford: Clarendon Press, 1870.
Pole, Reginald, *Pole's Defense of the Unity of the Church*, (translated by Joseph G. Dwyer), Westminster, Maryland: The Newman Press, 1965.
Pollard, A. F., *Tudor Tracts 1532–1588*, Westminster: A. Constable & Co., 1903.
Pollard, A. F., *Wolsey*, London: Longmans, Green & Co., 1929.
Quinsonas, Le Compte E. de, *Materiaux pour servir à l'histoire de Marguerite d'Autriche, Duchesse de Savoie, Regente des Pays-Bas*, Paris: Delaroque Frères, 1860.
The Receyt of the Ladie Kateryne, (edited by Gordon Kipling), Oxford: Oxford University Press, 1990.
Reiffenberg, Le Baron de (editor), *Chronique métrique de Chastellain et de Molinet, avec des notices sur ces auteurs et des remarques sur le texte corrigé*, Brussels: J.M. Lacrosse, 1836.
Ridley, Jasper, *The Love Letters of Henry VIII*, London: Cassell, 1988.
Robinson, Hastings, (editor), *Original Letters Relative to the English Reformation, Written During the Reigns of King Henry VIII, King Edward VI, and Queen Mary, Chiefly From the Archives of Zurich*, Cambridge: Cambridge University Press (for The Parker Society), 1846.

Rodocanachi, Emmanuel, *Une protectrice de la Réforme en Italie et en France, Renée de France, Duchesse de Ferrare*, Paris: Paul Ollendorff, 1896.

Roper, William, *The Life of Sir Thomas More by His Son-in-Law*, (edited by S.W. Singer), Chiswick: C. Whittingham, 1817.

Sadlack, Erin A., *The French Queen's Letters: Mary Tudor Brandon and the Politics of Marriage in Sixteenth-Century Europe*, New York: Palgrave Macmillan, 2011.

Sander, Nicholas, *Rise and Growth of the Anglican Schism*, (translated by David Lewis), London: Burns & Oates, 1877.

Sergeant, Philip W., *Anne Boleyn*, London: Hutchinson & Co. Ltd., 1924.

Spelman, Henry, *The English Works of Sir Henry Spelman, Kt, Publish'd in His Life-time; Together with His Posthumous Works, Relating to the Laws and Antiquities of England*, London: printed for D. Browne, 1723.

Spelman, John, *The Reports of Sir John Spelman*, (edited by J. H. Baker), London: Selden Society, 1977–1978.

Starkey, David, (editor), *Henry VIII: A European Court in England*, New York: Cross River Press, 1991.

Starkey, David, *Six Wives: The Queens of Henry VIII,* London: Chatto & Windus, 2003.

State Papers, King Henry the Eighth, London: published under the authority of His Majesty's Commission, 1831–1852.

The Statutes of the Realm. Printed by command of His Majesty King George the Third, in pursuance of an address of The House of Commons of Great Britain from original records and authentic manuscripts, London, 1810–1828.

Strickland, Agnes, *Lives of the Queens of England*, Philadelphia: Blanchard & Lea, 1856.

Stow, John & Howes, Edmund, *Annales, Or A General Chronicle of England*, London: Richard Meighen, 1631.

Stow, John, *The Survey of London, containing the originall, antiquitie, moderne estate, and description of that Citie*, London, 1603.

Strype, John, *Ecclesiastical Memorials*, Oxford: Clarendon Press, 1822.

Tanaka, Hidemichi, 'Leonardo da Vinci, Architect of Chambord?', *Artibus et Historiae*, Vol. 13, No. 25 (1992), pp. 85–102.

Thomas, William, *The Pilgrim: A Dialogue of the Life and Actions of King Henry the Eighth*, (edited by J. A. Froude), London: Parker, Son, & Bourn, 1861.

Thurley, Simon, *Houses of Power: The Places That Shaped the Tudor World*, London: Bantam Press, 2017.

Thurley, Simon, *The Royal Palaces of Tudor England: Architecture and Court Life 1460 – 1547*, New Haven: Yale University Press, 1993.

Turner, Sharon, *The History of England: From the Earliest Period to the Death of Elizabeth*, London: Longman, Orme, Brown, Green, & Longmans, 1839.

Twysden, Roger, *An Account of Queen Anne Boleyn: From a MS. in the Hand Writing of Sir Roger Twysden, Bart., 1623*, (edited by Robert Triphook), London, 1808.

Warnicke, Retha M., 'Anne Boleyn's Childhood and Adolescence', *The Historical Journal*, 28, 4, 1985.

Warnicke, Retha M., *The Rise and Fall of Anne Boleyn,* Cambridge: Cambridge University Press, 1989.

Weir, Alison, *The Lady in the Tower: The Fall of Anne Boleyn*, New York: Ballantine Books, 2010.

William of Malmesbury; *The History of the Kings of England and the Modern History of William of Malmesbury*, (translated by John Sharpe), London: Longman, Hurst, Rees, Orme, & Brown, 1815.

Wood, Mary Anne Everett, (editor), *Letters of Royal and Illustrious Ladies of Great Britain*, London: Henry Colburn, 1842.

Index

Acton Court 140, 141
Ahasuerus (Persian king) 154, 156, 157
Alwaye, Thomas 144
Amadas, Elizabeth 132–133
Anne of Brittany (Queen Consort of France) 33, 37
Ardres 41, 45
Arthur (Prince of England) 6, 7, 68, 76, 87, 88, 89
Avignon 77, 78
Aylmer, John (Bishop of London) 143

Bath Place 86
Barton, Elizabeth (The Nun of Kent) 120, 132
Battle of Bosworth 7, 66
Battle of Flodden Field 8
Beaufort, Margaret (Countess of Richmond) 18, 67, 122
Becket, Thomas (shrine of) 9
Betts, William 144
Beza, Théodore 142
Blickling Hall 4, 5
Blount, Elizabeth (Bessie) 58, 65
Boleyn, Anne (Marquess of Pembroke and Queen Consort of England) 3–4, 8–9, 10–11, 13–14, 15–21, 22, 23–24, 25, 27, 29–30, 31, 32, 33, 34, 36, 37, 38, 39, 43, 45, 46, 47, 48, 49–53, 58–60, 61, 62–63, 64–65, 68, 70, 71, 72, 76, 77, 78, 79, 80–83, 84, 85, 86, 91, 92, 93, 97, 98, 99, 101, 102, 104–105, 106, 107, 108–111, 112, 113, 114, 115–119, 120, 121–123, 124, 125, 126, 128–131, 132–135, 139, 140–141, 142, 143–146, 147–149, 151, 152, 153, 154, 156–158, 160, 161–168, 170, 172–176, 177, 179, 180, 181
Boleyn, Anne (née Hoo) 5
Boleyn, Dionisia 5
Boleyn, Elizabeth (née Howard) (Countess of Wiltshire) 3, 60, 64, 81, 98, 118, 125, 131, 178
Boleyn, Elizabeth (née Wood) 167
Boleyn, Geoffrey 4–5, 6
Boleyn, George (Viscount Rochford) 3, 4, 9, 10, 71, 92, 108, 111, 120, 125, 129, 131, 134, 150–151, 161, 164–165, 166, 167, 168–169, 170–171, 174, 176
Boleyn, Henry (son of Thomas Boleyn, Earl of Wiltshire) 3
Boleyn, Jane (née Parker) (Lady Rochford) 111, 118, 165, 178
Boleyn, Margaret (née Butler) 5, 47
Boleyn, Thomas (son of Geoffrey Boleyn) 5
Boleyn, Thomas (son of Thomas Boleyn, Earl of Wiltshire) 3
Boleyn, Thomas (Earl of Wiltshire) 3, 4, 5–6, 7, 8, 9, 11, 13, 15, 17–18, 19, 21, 22, 23, 29–30, 47, 48, 59–60, 70–71, 78, 89, 108, 116, 125, 129, 131, 154, 155, 177–178, 179
Boleyn, William 5
Bosch, Hieronymus 22
Boulogne 109
Bourbon, Nicholas 143, 144
Bouton, Claude de (Lord of Corbaron) 15, 18
Brandon, Anne 20
Brandon, Frances 60
Brandon, Charles (Duke of Suffolk) 13, 20, 27, 32, 35–37, 41, 60, 78, 90, 97, 108, 116, 155, 174, 177
Brenz, Johannes 143
Brereton, William 164, 166–167, 171–172, 175
Bridewell Palace 86, 87
Brooke, Elizabeth 53, 63
Brown, George 112
Browne, Anthony 166, 177
Browne, Elizabeth (Countess of Worcester) 166
Brussels 19, 25
Bryan, Francis 153
Bulleux, Hugues de 20

Bulleux, Mademoiselle de 20
Butler, James 48, 49, 60, 61
Butler, Piers 47–48, 49
Butler, Thomas (Seventh Earl of Ormond) 5, 47, 61
Butts, William 82, 83, 144

Calais 41, 86, 108, 109, 111, 120, 129, 141, 163, 164, 173
Cambrai, Court of 15, 16, 25
Cambridge University 6, 129, 144, 158
Camden, William 3, 4
Campeggio, Lorenzo (Cardinal) 85, 86–87, 88, 89, 90, 91, 97
Canterbury Cathedral 9
Carew, Nicholas 153, 154, 177, 178
Carey, Eleanor 83–84
Carey, Henry (Lord Hunsdon) 65, 83, 179
Carey, Katherine 65, 83, 179
Carey, Mary (née Boleyn) 3, 4, 9, 10, 13, 31, 32, 37, 39, 58, 65, 70, 71, 78, 111, 118, 131, 170, 179
Carey, William 65, 83, 131
Carthusian monks 140
Castel Sant'Angelo 75, 80
Castle Tervuren 17, 19, 25
Catherine of Austria (Queen Consort of Portugal) 19
Cavendish, George 63
Chabot, Philippe (Admiral De Brion) 134–135
Chapuys, Eustace 99–100, 101, 109, 114, 121, 124, 125, 129, 131, 134, 140, 147, 149–151, 156–157, 165, 174, 176
Charles of Valois (Duke of Angoulême) 134
Charles V (Holy Roman Emperor) 13, 19, 21, 25, 27, 29, 57, 72, 74, 75, 76, 77, 78, 79, 80, 85, 99, 114, 118, 120, 121, 124, 133, 149–150, 151, 157
Charles VIII (King of France) 11
Christian II (King of Denmark) 25, 27, 28
Claude (Queen Consort of France) 33, 37, 38, 39, 43, 44, 45, 48, 60, 109, 111
Clement VII (Pope) 74–75, 77, 78, 79–80, 86, 87, 88, 90, 93, 97, 99, 101, 103, 104, 105, 113, 120, 133, 150, 151
Cobham, Anne 128
Columbus, Christopher 24
Constantine X (Byzantine emperor) 119
Cortona, Domenico da 38

Coudenberg, Palace of 25, 26
Court of Cambrai 15, 16, 25
Court of Savoy 16, 19, 22–25
Courtenay, Henry (Marquess of Exeter) 108, 155, 177, 178
Cranmer, Thomas (Archbishop of Canterbury) 102–103, 114, 115, 124, 163, 170, 177, 178
Cromwell, Thomas 97, 103, 104, 107, 111, 131, 149–150, 151, 153, 154–157, 161, 162, 163, 170, 171, 174, 177, 178

Da Vinci, Leonardo 38, 43
Defence of the Seven Sacraments, The 91
d'Étaples, Jacques Lefevre 143, 146
Dormer, Jane (Duchess of Feria) 3
Dover 13, 17, 77, 107, 157

Edenbridge 4
Edward I (King of England) 7
Edward III (King of England) 129
Edward IV (King of England) 6, 129
Edward VI (King of England) 177, 178
Eleanor of Aquitaine (Queen Consort of France and of England) 53, 181
Eleanor of Austria (Queen Consort of Portugal and of France) 13, 19, 21, 25, 109–110
Elizabeth of York (Queen Consort of England) 18, 34, 66, 67, 89, 125
Elizabeth I (Queen Regnant of England) 33, 123, 124–126, 132, 133, 134, 147, 157–158, 160, 172, 177, 178, 179–181
Esther (queen of King Ahasuerus) 154, 156–157
Eustace (Count of Boulogne) 6

Felipez, Francisco 74
Ferdinand of Aragon (King of Spain) 6, 11, 104
Ferdinand of Austria (Holy Roman Emperor) 19
Field of the Cloth of Gold 41–45, 57, 63
Fish, Simon 92–93, 144
Fisher, John (Bishop of Rochester) 77, 88, 139, 140
Fitzroy, Henry (Duke of Richmond) 65, 66, 67, 108, 165, 174
Foix, Françoise de (Countess of Châteaubriant) 39
Fontainebleau 49

Forman, Thomas 144
Fox, Edward 79–80, 82, 102
Francis I (King of France) 31–32, 35, 37–39, 41, 43–46, 49, 57, 71, 108, 109, 111, 129, 131, 135
Francis of Valois (son of Francis I) 39

Gainsford, Anne 128
Gardiner, Stephen (Bishop of Winchester) 79–80, 82, 102, 108
Giustiniani, Sebastiano 41, 43
Gontier, Palamedes 135
Gray's Inn 92
Greenwich Palace 49, 72, 81–82, 105, 107, 115, 120, 121, 126, 147, 161
Grey, Margaret (née Wotton) (Marchioness of Dorset) 124
Grey, Thomas (Marquess of Dorset) 89
Gossaert, Jan (Mabuse) 22
Guevara, Diégo de 16
Guînes (Guisnes) 41, 43, 44, 45

Haman (Persian minister) 154, 157
Hampton Court 58, 98, 106, 107, 177, 179
Harold (King of England) 119
Haute, Jane 3, 51
Hayes, Cornelius 129
Heptameron 38
Heneage, Thomas 112
Henry I (King of England) 66
Henry II (King of England) 53, 180
Henry V (King of England) 129
Henry VI (King of England) 6, 66
Henry VII (King of England) 6, 8, 18, 58, 66, 67, 76, 89, 104, 141
Henry VIII (King of England) 3, 6–7, 11, 13, 18, 27, 29, 30, 36, 39–41, 43–44, 45, 46, 48, 49, 57–58, 59, 60, 61, 62–63, 64–66, 67, 68, 70, 71, 72, 73, 74, 76, 77, 78, 79, 80–81, 82, 83, 84, 85, 86, 87, 88, 89, 90, 91, 92–93, 97, 98–99, 100, 101, 102, 120–121, 122, 123, 124, 125, 126, 128, 129, 130, 131, 132, 133, 134, 135, 154, 157, 158, 160, 161, 162, 163, 165, 166, 167, 168, 169, 170, 171, 172, 173, 174, 175, 176, 177, 178, 179, 180, 181
Henry VIII (play) 62
Henry of Valois (Duke of Orléans) 71
Hever 4
Hever Castle 8, 9, 61, 63, 64, 82, 85, 86

Holbein, Hans 49, 72, 118, 126
Holland, Bess 128
Hoo, Thomas (Baron Hoo and Hastings) 5
Horenbout, Gerard 23
Horenbout, Lucas 23, 129
Horenbout, Susanna 23
Howard, Agnes (née Tilney) (Duchess of Norfolk) 114, 118, 124
Howard, Henry (Earl of Surrey) 167, 168, 174, 178
Howard, John (First Duke of Norfolk) 7
Howard, Katheryn (Queen Consort of England) 165
Howard, Mary (Duchess of Richmond) 114, 115
Howard, Thomas (Earl of Surrey and Second Duke of Norfolk) 7–8, 61
Howard, Thomas (Earl of Surrey and Third Duke of Norfolk) 48, 78, 97, 108, 112, 128, 149, 161, 167, 169, 177
Hunne, Richard 90, 91, 92

Isabella of Castile (Queen Regnant of Spain) 6, 11–12, 18, 87
Isabeau of Austria (Queen Consort of Denmark) 13, 19, 21, 25, 27, 28, 50

James IV (King of Scotland) 7, 8
John of Asturias (Prince of Spain) 11, 24
Jordan, Isabel 83–84

Katherine of Aragon (Queen Consort of England) 6–7, 18, 23, 39, 41, 43, 44, 45, 57, 58, 59, 60, 65–66, 67, 68, 71, 72, 73–74, 76–77, 78, 79, 80–81, 85, 86–88, 89, 90, 93, 97, 99–100, 101–102, 103, 104, 105, 106–107, 109, 110, 114–115, 118, 121, 124, 125, 126, 128, 129, 132, 133, 134, 139, 147, 149, 152, 170
Kingston, Mary (née Scrope) 167
Kingston, William 116, 120, 161–162, 163, 164, 170–171, 172–174, 176, 177
Knight, William 77–78, 79

La Veure (Tervuren) 17, 19, 21, 25
Latimer, Hugh 144, 146
Latymer, William 48, 144
Lee, Rowland 112
Leicester Abbey 99
Leti, Gregorio 61–62

Lincoln's Inn 5, 6
London 5, 6, 77, 86, 91, 99, 107, 119, 140, 176, 179
Louis VII (King of France) 53
Louis XII (King of France) 27, 29, 31, 32, 33, 34, 35, 36, 37
Louise of Savoy 37, 45

Margaret of Angoulême 38, 45, 91, 110, 142–143, 144
Margaret of Austria 4, 11–14, 15–25, 29–30, 43, 46, 48, 60, 63, 85
Margaret of York 22
Margaret (Queen Consort of Scotland) 7
Marshall, Mistress 128
Mary (Queen Consort of France and Duchess of Suffolk) 23, 27, 29, 30, 31–32, 34–37, 41, 50, 52, 89, 118, 125
Mary I (Queen Regnant of England) 11, 39, 44, 66, 67, 68, 71–72, 133–134, 139–140, 151, 152, 165, 172, 177, 178, 179
Mary of Austria/Mary of Hungary (Queen Consort of Hungary) 13, 19, 21, 25
Mary of Burgundy 11
Marye, Mistress 144
Maude (Matilda) (Princess of England and Empress Consort of the Holy Roman Empire) 66, 67
Maximilian I (Holy Roman Emperor) 11, 12, 16, 19, 24, 43, 57
Mechelen (Malines) 16, 19, 20, 21–22, 24, 85
Mendoza, Inigo de 72–73, 74
More, The 106
More, Thomas 98, 103, 140

Norris, Henry 112, 158, 160, 161, 163, 164, 166–167, 171
Notre Dame Cathedral 32

Orvieto 79
Oxford University 144

Page, Richard 164, 166
Paget, Hugh 4, 16, 20
Paris 31–33, 36, 46, 86
Percy, Henry (Fifth Earl of Northumberland) 61

Percy, Henry (Sixth Earl of Northumberland) 60–61, 63, 76, 99, 155, 167, 168, 170
Philibert II (Duke of Savoy) 12
Philip I (King of Castile) 13
Philip the Good (Duke of Burgundy) 22
Plantagenet, Arthur (Lord Lisle) 120, 155, 175
Philippa of Hainault (Queen Consort of England) 129, 130
Pole, Reginald (Archbishop of Canterbury) 68, 69
Poppea (Empress Consort of Rome) 70
Poyntz, Nicholas 141, 177

Renée of France (Duchess of Ferrara) 32–33, 34, 37, 76
Richard III (King of England) 6, 8, 66
Richmond Palace 78, 79
Rochester, Magdalen 20
Rohan, Pierre de (Marshal of France) 37
Roo, John 92

Saint Denis, Church of 31–32
Saint Paul's Cathedral 7
Saint Peter, Church of (Mechelen) 22
Saint Peter, Church of (Rome) 75
Saint Peter Ad Vincula, Church of 176
Saint Rumbold's Cathedral 21–22, 25
Salinas, Maria de (Baroness Willoughby de Eresby) 147
Sampson, Richard 93
Shelton, Madge 128, 164
Semmonet 17
Seymour, Edward 142, 152, 153, 177, 178
Seymour, Jane (Queen Consort of England) 128, 141, 151–153, 157, 170, 174, 177
Seymour, John 141
Shaxton, Nicholas 144, 162–163
Skip, John 144, 154, 158, 162, 172
Smeaton, Mark 163–164, 166, 172
Stafford, Edward (Duke of Buckingham) 58
Stafford, William 131
Stephen (King of England) 66
Strand, The 58, 86
Strickland, Agnes 8, 70
Supplication for the Beggars, A 92

Tarbes, Bishop of 76
Tower Hill 171, 174

Tower of London 99, 109, 114, 115, 116–117, 161, 163, 164, 167, 168, 170, 173, 174–176
Twysden, Roger 3, 142
Tyndale, William 92, 93, 144, 146

Valladolid 74
Van Eyck, Jan 22
Vendôme, Madame de 110

Walsingham (shrine of) 9, 112, 114
Walsingham, Edmund 116
Warham, William (Archbishop of Canterbury) 77, 114
Warnicke, Retha 20
West, Nicholas (Bishop of Ely) 90
West, Thomas (Baron De La Warr) 180
Westminster Abbey 109, 115, 119, 180
Weston, Francis 164, 166, 172
Whitehall Palace (York Place) 59, 98, 107, 112, 164, 180
William I (King of England) 6
Willoughby, Antony 89–90
Wiltshire, Bridget (Lady Wingfield) 166
Wolfhall 141
Wolsey, Thomas (Cardinal and Archbishop of York) 27, 41, 45, 46, 47, 48, 49, 58, 59, 60, 61, 62, 63, 64, 68, 72–73, 74, 76, 77–79, 80, 81, 83–84, 86, 88, 89, 90, 91, 92, 93, 97–99, 103, 106, 107, 144, 157
Wyatt, Elizabeth (née Brooke) 53
Wyatt, George 3, 51–52, 80, 107
Wyatt, Thomas 50, 52–53, 63, 112, 164, 166